# The Peon Book

## How to Manage Us

**Dave Haynes**

BERRETT-KOEHLER PUBLISHERS, INC.
San Francisco

**Berrett-Koehler Publishers, Inc.**
235 Montgomery Street, Suite 650
San Francisco, CA 94104-2916
Tel: (415) 288-0260 Fax: (415) 362-2512 www.bkconnection.com

**Ordering Information**
**Quantity sales.** Special discounts are available on quantity purchases by corporations, associations, and others. For details, contact the "Special Sales Department" at the Berrett-Koehler address above.
**Individual sales.** Berrett-Koehler publications are available through most bookstores. They can also be ordered directly from Berrett-Koehler:
Tel: (800) 929-2929; Fax: (802) 864-7626; www.bkconnection.com
**Orders for college textbook/course adoption use.** Please contact Berrett-Koehler: Tel: (800) 929-2929; Fax: (802) 864-7626.
**Orders by U.S. trade bookstores and wholesalers.** Please contact Publishers Group West, 1700 Fourth Street, Berkeley, CA 94710.
Tel: (510) 528-1444; Fax (510) 528-3444.

Berrett-Koehler and the BK logo are registered trademarks of Berrett-Koehler Publishers, Inc.

Printed in the United States of America
Berrett-Koehler books are printed on long-lasting acid-free paper. When it is available, we choose paper that has been manufactured by environmentally responsible processes. These may include using trees grown in sustainable forests, incorporating recycled paper, minimizing chlorine in bleaching, or recycling the energy produced at the paper mill.

**Library of Congress Cataloging-in-Publication Data**

Haynes, Dave 1975-
        The peon book: how to manage us / by Dave Haynes.
            p. cm.
        Includes index.
        ISBN 1-57675-285-2
        1. Management. I. Title.
        HD31.H394 2003
        658.4'09—dc22            2003063841

First Edition
08 07 06 05 04            10 9 8 7 6 5 4 3 2 1

# Contents

**Preface**      vi

**Introduction**      1
A Change of Focus

**1. Get Trustworthy**      11
Do it for the Peon
Communication
Two-faced

**2. Get Real**      31
Empathy
Remember

**3. Get Personal**      53
Treat People Like They Are People
Make Their Goals Your Goals
The Naysayers
Treat People Like You Are People

**4. Get In The Trenches**      79
"I'd like to see you do this."
Creative Performing

**5. Get Feedback**      113
Run with It
Check Engine

**6. Get Organized**      126
Create the Vision
Flavor of the Month
Keep it All Together
Conclusion

**Index**      151

**About the Author**      153

# The Peon Book

One day my boss pulled me into her office. We had just seen some people on our team leave the company due to basic unhappiness, and the boss asked me for . . . . .

## Preface

. . . . .**my take on what was going on**. Why is everybody unhappy? Why is employee morale so low? We work in a large company with great benefits and pension plans; why are these people leaving? Could it be that we hired the wrong people, or is it something that is going on here at work?

I was caught somewhat off guard by the questions, so I told my boss that I would think about it and get back to her. While sucking in fumes from other cars during my rush hour commute home, I started to note in my mind the things that my company could do to help people be happier, more motivated, and more dedicated in their jobs. The next morning, I woke up early and started to jot down those reasons. I came up with quite a long list, and before long I said to myself, "I could write a freaking book about all the things this company could do better." So, I started to write a book.

I soon realized that the problems that existed in my company were the same problems we had at my previous workplace. After thinking about it a little further, I realized that in fact these problems were common in almost all the organizations in which I had been involved. The funny thing is that most of them weren't really problems; they were merely situations in which everyone was focused on the wrong things. Specifically, it seemed that while management's intentions were good, they still got results the opposite of those intended—because management focused on the wrong things.

For example, it used to drive me nuts that managers would come in with these great, gung ho programs to get us going, but would then neglect some of the fundamental issues that really hindered their ability to lead and our desire to follow. That is like putting supreme gasoline in my old clunker truck—better gas alone is not going to help my car run better. Many other, fundamental issues need to be addressed before the high performance fuel is going to make a difference.

I assume that the reason so many managers focus on the wrong thing has to do with the fact that they are getting their information from the wrong sources. Just as many people who make decisions about marketing a product have never talked to a customer, many managers get their ideas without ever talking to their employees.

I intend to change that. Unlike most other management/self-help book on bookshelves today, this book is written by a peon. It will allow you to see the world through the eyes of an insider, rather than those of some outsider.

Some may ask, Why the word *peon*? Why not *valued team member or synergistic contributor*? The word peon originally described a certain class of people; some would say that it still does. However, I would argue that peonage is a state of mind. It is a situation in which we feel like we have no control over what is being done. We feel powerless. We are just doing what the boss tells us.

Some may feel that way at work. Others may feel powerful at work, and then become a peon when they get home. You may think that a company owner or CEO is not a peon, but if you ask those people, they'll tell you that they feel like a peon in relation to their creditors or shareholders. Because so many relationships exist in society, it is safe to say that each one of us, in some capacity or another, is a peon. Don't be afraid of it; it's not a bad thing. Embrace your inner peon. It is part of life. It is the way our societies are set up.

However, because each of us is a peon in some form or another, we can also conclude that each of us is a manager in some form or another. We are a manager in the sense that someone else likely feels they are our peon. Possibly you are a peon at work all day but then, when you get home, you are the president of your homeowners association. Maybe you make no decisions at work, but when you get home you make all the decisions for yourself and your spouse.

If peonage is a state of mind, so is Manager—the kind with a capital $M$. It is human nature to become a capital $M$ manager once responsibility has been placed on one's shoulders; one has to be much more focused and aware in order to become a lowercase $m$ manager. This book is about helping you become a lowercase $m$ manager. Why would you want to do that? Because it will help you develop a relationship with your peons that inspires them to be happy, and happy employees are productive employees. They are employees that feel loyal to your company. They are employees that stay.

Unlike traditional boring management books, I have written this book in a funny, lighthearted way. You shouldn't fall asleep reading this book nor get to the end of a chapter and say to yourself, "Okay, now what did I just read?" It can also come across as a bit sarcastic or mean. That is intentional, because that is how we, as your employees, often feel. The sarcasm comes from frustration. You may not think that your employees feel like peons, or that you are one of those Managers; however, it still exists in people's minds. They still feel like peons.

I am not the only person who feels this way. If you really want an insight into how your employees feel, read this book. As I stated earlier, the issues I noticed in my company exist at almost all the organizations in which I have worked, from mom-and-pop to Fortune 500 companies. Chances are, if one of your peons accidentally picked up this book and started reading it, they would start saying to themselves, "Oh, yeah. My manager is like this" or "I've had a manager just like that at a previous job." All organizations have a Management-peon structure in place. I'm giving you the chance to make it, instead, a peon-management relationship. Take advantage of it.

## Acknowledgments

I'd like to first thank Drex and Quin for giving me the confidence to do this, and for setting a powerful example of walking the talk when it comes to following your dreams. You are both brass elephants. As Quin showed me, pursuit of your life's destiny starts with a simple choice. You both inspire us all to live the spirit of FDM.

Second, I'd like to personally thank all the staff at Berrett-Koehler Publishers for taking a chance on some no-name goofball. Steve, thanks for establishing an organization where people can make choices based on moral obligations. And Jeevan, thanks for your desire to instigate social change from the inside.

I would also like to thank God for being kind enough to bless me with talents. I only hope that He is satisfied with how I am developing them.

And last but most, I'd like to thank my beautiful wife, Lorette, and my wonderful children. You are my inspiration for everything I do. You have always helped me keep things in the right perspective and to see the world with a different eye.

☾

Dave Haynes
Phoenix
January 2004

# A Change of Focus

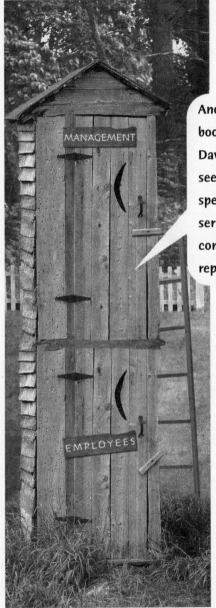

Another management book? Who is this guy, Dave Haynes? I've never seen him as the keynote speaker at a lecture series, or presenting his company's year-end report to . . . . .

## Introduction

. . . . . **Wall Street**. Who is he? Some Harvard professor, some expert on synergy, some business psychologist? Not exactly. In reality, not even remotely.

I am Dave Haynes, and I am a peon. I am a worker, a scrub, a subordinate. I hold no distinguished title, I don't have a special business card, and my office is a cube. I am not embarrassed by this; it is simply a fact. I have not successfully climbed any corporate ladder. I have not spent hours in a lab researching employee blood pressure levels in a work environment. I don't have time for that; I am too busy working. Too busy slaving away for some company somewhere, trying to put bread on the table and a little money in the bank. Too busy driving in rush hour traffic and preserving my remaining vacation days.

So why would I, an underqualified peon, write a book about management? And what can some underclassman tell you about managing your team? That's a very good question. Let me answer with a scenario.

Let's say you set out to train a dog. You have three options for sources on how to train that dog. The first is a training manual written by a PhD in dog psychology who has spent many hours observing dogs being trained. She tours the country giving motivational seminars on dog training and sells millions of copies of her dog-training books. The second option is an experienced dog trainer who has a proven record of training success. He once trained a dog that won top prize at the Westminster Kennel Club Dog Show, and he brought a dog from the brink of death to being a top breeder. The third choice would be the option to actually talk to the dog, to know its thoughts and wishes, to have a frank conversation with the animal about how it prefers that you train it.

Which would you rather have? I'd much rather get the information straight from the dog. How invaluable would it be for your dog to be able to tell you, "Look, Buddy, you're a nice guy and all, but the doggie biscuit thing just ain't workin'. You call that a reward? Come on. Calamari! That's what I really want; that's the key to getting me to do all those stupid tricks. You feed me calamari, and I'll dance the Macarena. Whatever you want me to do, reward me with calamari, and I'll do it."

If calamari is indeed the key to complete obedience when training a dog, how else would you discover that than by talking to the dog itself? Only the dog would know that. The experienced dog trainer wouldn't know that, and the PhD certainly wouldn't know it, but the dog would.

Since many employees feel like they are asked to sit, beg, and roll over on a regular basis, and since many managers feel like they are taming a bunch of animals, I figure it isn't too much of a stretch to draw the comparison here between dog/trainer and peon/manager. How valuable would it be for you as a manager to be able to hear honestly—and I mean completely honestly—what your employees are thinking?

Sure the company has open door policies and employee satisfaction surveys, but you and I know such measures are like telling your neighbor "If you need any help, let me know" when you see him pull up with a new piano. You probably don't really want to help; in fact, you offer your help, knowing darn well he isn't going to ask, just because it is the right thing to do. Similarly, surveys and open door policies are not getting you accurate employee feedback.

How valuable to your success as a leader would honest, effective feedback be? How would you benefit by knowing exactly how your team evaluates your management style? Don't tell me that they are already up-front with you. If you think your relationship with your employees is that good, that they tell you everything without holding anything back, then I would tell you to go get the milk, because it's time to pour you a bowl of Reality Cereal.

Have you ever wondered what your people talk about around the watercooler, or in the restroom, or in the parking lot next to their cars? Sure, they bring up the last episode of some TV show when you are around, but the minute you leave, don't think for a minute that the conversation stays the same. Once you are gone, they are probably talking about you. Think about it: When you get around other managers, what do you talk about? You spread gossip about subordinates and you spend a lot of time talking about your own boss. We peons aren't any different.

"They talk about me?" you ask. "Really? What do they say?"

Well, first we talk about your terrible haircut, then we discuss matters of personal hygiene... Just kidding. Actually, most of the time we analyze your management skills—or lack thereof.

"I can't believe he wrote that e-mail. Does he not have a clue about what we are already doing?"

"Man, I don't trust her. She seems like she'd stab you in the back."

"My manager is so cool; she took us all out to breakfast this morning."

"Aw, man. My manager would never do that… You know him: Mr. Corporate Guy."

Believe it. Your subordinates talk about you and analyze your management skills. It's a fact of life—and one of the great rights of being a peon. But don't get all depressed and down on yourself, thinking it's all negative. We do notice when you do something right. It's usually followed with, "Let's see how long that lasts," but at least we notice.

So why am I telling you this? Why tell you what the peons expect? Why don't I just get back to work and leave things the way they are? For my own personal reasons, I have decided to break ranks, to be an informant, a snitch. I have seen too many good people show up day in and day out for a job that could be rewarding but isn't. And I've seen too many managers try very hard, only to find they are spinning their wheels.

In truth, I want to help those managers be more effective and more centered on their employees. I want to tell all the managers in the world what it is we peons expect them to do, how we peons expect to be treated, how it is possible to get us peons to actually work. We may be peons but you don't have to treat us that way, and frankly, we feel that you do. If you could learn how not to treat us like peons—and actually change your ways—I guarantee you would see a difference in your team's productivity, happiness, and subsequent loyalty to your company. It's really not that difficult, and my suggestions aren't going to be anything earth-shattering, but the suggestions will be brought to you from a different point of view, helping you to see management with a valuable change of focus.

One of my sisters studied biology in college. One day she and I were talking about her schooling, and she informed me that in order for rabbits to fully digest their food, they double-digest it. In other words, rabbits eat their own poop.

Another sister was privy to the conversation. Her reply to this revelation of fact about rabbit feces was, "That is so gross! I will never kiss a rabbit again!"

My response was a little different: "No way! They turn on their own diggity? I want to see that! Why do they eat their own poop? All this time I've been around rabbits and never noticed. That is amazing!"

My sister and I received the same information, but we came to completely different conclusions. Our individual focus pointed us in totally different directions regarding rabbits turning around and eating their own little pebbles. In order to learn more about a rabbit's digestive patterns, then, my sister would need to change her focus to be more like mine. In order to see the disgusting nature of this rabbit deed, I would need to change my focus to be more like hers.

What does a rabbit offal have to do with management? Everything! One's focus can be crucial to one's ability to interpret the world. Many managers are doing a good job, but if they changed their focus just a little bit and saw the situation from a different angle, they would turn themselves into great managers, well-loved managers, and promotion-worthy managers.

For this reason, I have put together some suggestions for managers, from the peon's perspective. Not from the perspective of some PhD or "successful" manager, but straight from the horse's—or dog's, or maybe even rabbit's—mouth. If all managers concentrated on these suggestions, their relationship with their subordinates would improve and they would be able to get more of what they want out of these subordinates.

In order to make these suggestions easier to remember, I've created a list of *get* statements:

**Get trustworthy**

**Get real**

**Get personal**

**Get in the trenches**

**Get feedback**

**Get organized**

Get it? I heard somewhere that our minds can remember any pattern as long as it contains less than seven items. That's why there are seven numbers in a phone number and "seven habits of highly effective people." There are even seven wonders of the world. But I have gone one better: I am only going to make you remember six suggestions. I realize that the first letters of the second words don't make some catchy remember-all word (unless you can make something out of TRPT-FO), but I think they should still be easy to remember, even for you senior managers.

You might ask yourself if these suggestions are totally new and revolutionary. Probably not. Will they make you the greatest manager of all time? Maybe. They are simply suggestions that, if used correctly, can help you to be a great manager. They are things I have identified, through my countless appearances on the peon stage, as things that would have helped my managers to manage better. That is not to say I thought they were terrible managers, only to say that, with a little tweaking and the right focus, they could have been more effective, and they could have gotten more out of me.

I hope that by this point you have started to feel that it might benefit you to listen to what a peon has to say, that it might help you change your focus. But why should Dave Haynes tell you about improving the peon experience? Who am I to be the voice of peons? The answer is that I am a card-carrying peon, and I have been one for a long time. I am not a manager, but rather one of the managed. I look at my shoes when I walk, I work in a cube, I bring my lunch to work—I am a peon.

Perhaps *peon* is a politically incorrect term; I should probably call *us managerial-title–challenged contributors*. Since I am a peon, though, the ethics of political correctness allow me to call myself a peon. It's okay for fellow peons to refer to themselves as peons in contexts such as "What's up, peon?" or "Hey, peon. Get me a pencil" or "I am such a peon." However, proper peon etiquette dictates that if you are not a peon, you may not go around smacking off the P-word. Management should never—ever—call us peons.

I am an expert in everything about being a peon because I have spent my whole life as a peon. As one of eight children, I was one of my parents' peons. From the age of fourteen, I have held jobs in just about every field, from mowing lawns, to sales, to marketing, to bus driving, to lifeguarding, to rabbit re-feeding. I also have worked in all kinds of organizations—mom-and-pop businesses, large public corporations, nonprofits, government agencies—and while I don't know what goes on in every department in every business in every industry, I have noticed that certain things tend to remain the same, and that the relationship between managers and employees generally needs a refocus, no matter where you go.

Like any suggestion, the power to act is in the recipient. You may read this book and say to yourself, "This is the biggest pile of tripe I've ever read," and then run each page through the shredder. Twice. Or you may read it and say, "If I were a rabbit, I'd probably turn around and eat my feces too." Or, if you are a good manager, you will say, "Wow! Is this really how my peons feel about me? I need to change." In any case, it's up to you to do something.

Knowledge itself is useless; knowledge that motivates to action is wisdom.

I hope you are wiser for reading this book.

☾

# Get Trustworthy

Welcome to the world of the peon. Please keep your hands and arms in the car, and make sure that your seat backs are in the vertical position. Pregnant women and people with . . . . .

## Chapter One

..... **weak constitutions should sit this one out.** The view of the world through the eyes of a peon is not always a clear or peaceful one, but it is the key to your success as a manager. My intent is to help you transform yourself into a better leader by letting you know how we peons think and what we expect from you.

In order to make a successful transformation, though, you and I are going to have to establish some ground rules. First, I promise to be completely honest with you, that I will not hold anything back. I also promise that I will not just diagnose problems but also will give you solutions to those problems. I promise to keep the book as entertaining as possible for a business book, and I promise to give you real suggestions that you can use in your job today.

In return, I expect a few things from you. First, I expect you to be open-minded. Yes, I am a peon, and yes, my clothes are less expensive than yours, and no, I don't have a talking GPS system in my car, but you still might learn something from me. Second, I expect you to be honest with yourself. Nobody is here except you and me, and I want you to be honest in your self-assessments. Third, I expect you to laugh. Don't take my jokes too seriously—I don't. Finally, I expect you to do something with these suggestions. If you are just reading this to appease someone else, then put it down and go back to riding your NordicTrack. I want you to plan to get something out of these suggestions that will help you be a better manager.

Now that we are on the same page, ready to help you be a more peon-friendly manager, the first thing we need to address is your personality. I am aware that changing personality traits is like jamming toothpicks under your fingernails. I realize that we all read books that tell us "be a better listener" or "be your own motivator"—things that are easier said than done. We are who we are, and reading some stupid book isn't going to change who we are, is it?

No, a book is not going to change you, but it can point out some traits to refocus. I know what I just said about the toothpicks, but stick with me. If certain personality traits aren't established as the basis of our new, managerial you, then the rest won't work. In the words of Jesus, quoted in the Gospel of Matthew, it will be a house built on sand that, when the rains come, will wash away.

In order to identify traits that need refocusing, it is important to point out that the two quickest ways to offend or insult another person are either to disrespect them or to deceive them. These can be very difficult offenses to forgive; in fact, in some cases, such behavior can lead the offended party to much more serious offenses, in retaliation. This book as a whole focuses on point number one; this chapter is about point number two.

Therefore, the first and most critical managerial trait is to be trustworthy. Any good relationship is established on a basis of trust: husband and wife, parent and child, manager and employee, CEO and investors. Trustworthiness is a significant personality trait; it is the glue of a relationship and it is the bond that makes a group a team. Trust is critical to the success of any personal or professional relationship, and if you want to get your employees to do anything, then they'd better trust you. Deceit is the fastest way to lose the respect of your peons. They will not be motivated to work for you if they do not trust you.

Trust is a funny thing, though. It is so easy to damage, and so difficult to repair. This funny world with all of its funny crooks and all their funny ideas have made us all a little gunshy when it comes to trusting others. Many managers assume that because they occupy a management position, people will automatically trust their judgment and look to them for leadership. As though just by placing the mantle of leadership on their shoulders they become a different person, and suddenly their subordinates trust them completely. Such an assumption is like assuming that simply because someone has a driver's license they should be trusted to drive your car.

We peons respect you as a manager because of your authority, but that doesn't necessarily mean we trust you. In fact, to most employees, the mere fact of a manager's ascension up the corporate ladder makes them about as trustworthy as the company's legal department. A manager can be trusted, but many elements other than just a title must be present. A title may get you respect, but it does not earn you any trust.

So your peons don't trust you—so what? No big deal... neither do your in-laws. Life moves on, right? Consider, however:

**Peons will only follow a leader wholeheartedly if they are completely confident in the promises made by that leader.**

An employee will hardly be confident in your promises if they mistrust you. I think every manager dreams that when they order their team to jump the unanimous response is "How high?" However, if your employees don't trust you, their response will be more like "Is there really any reason we need to jump? What if we hurt ourselves? Is this in my job description?" Peons won't have confidence in your vision if they don't trust you. A prospective shareholder won't have confidence in their stock purchase if they don't trust you. A prospective spouse won't have confidence in your plans for the future if they don't trust you.

Central to your new focus must be a desire to develop the trust of your peons. What have you done lately to gain their trust and confidence? Further, what have you done lately that may have violated that trust, even something that may not have affected your peons directly—something such as lying, cheating, or failing to keep a promise? If you want peons to follow you, be trustworthy. When we trust you, we will be confident in you and willing to follow you, because we won't fear that you are leading us in the wrong direction.

Years ago, I worked for a small manufacturer, selling water purification equipment for people's homes. Many of the salespeople in this field had come from the old school of door-to-door selling. Their sales philosophy consisted of a quick message, very little information, all kinds of promises, and some Zig Ziglar close to wrap up the deal. This type of salesperson never worried about future customer service; instead, it was "get the sale, get the praise, and get the commission." In other words, their professional behavior was successful but untrustworthy.

One of these old-school guys was a seasoned salesman who felt that he could sell pretty much anything to anybody, anytime. Within weeks of joining our company, he began selling the socks off every other salesperson. His commission checks were three times the amount of anyone else's; he was making some great money.

I started to watch him closely, to see what I could learn, because I wanted to make that kind of money. I noticed that he kept no real record of his customers and engaged in no follow-up. I didn't understand it. How could he care so little and yet sell so much? So one day I stopped him and asked him to enlighten me. His response was that his basic pitch was always the same, and that the point of the pitch was to give the customer enough information to know the general product they were buying, but nothing more. He felt letting a customer know too much was dangerous. That didn't sit well with me, but my opinion didn't matter; he was happy, the boss was happy, everybody was making money, so that was success, right?

However, I could sense the eventual backlash from this type of selling: the buyer's remorse and the increased customer expectations resulting from inflated promises, not to mention the ethical dilemmas presented by working this way. But the boss was so impressed by this guy's work that he basically demoted the current sales manager and gave Mr. Performance the job.

I didn't like this setup, so I went in to talk to the boss.

"Boss, I don't like Mr. Performance as my sales manager."

"Why not?"

"'Cause I don't trust him."

"Neither do I, but he's making this company a ton of money."

"Maybe so, but don't you see that this is going to come back and bite you in the butt?"

"What am I supposed to do? The other sales manager isn't doing a good job motivating you, and—"

"And you think this guy is going to motivate me? Motivate me to look for another job maybe."

"Fine. Go look for another job. This is the way it is."

As a result, I did start job searching, and when the right opportunity came up, I left.

Think about the ramifications of having an untrustworthy manager at the helm. Not only did he set a bad precedent for the company, but he also managed to demoralize the rest of the workforce at the company, beginning with me. My poor wife had to hear me rant and rave over dinner about this untrustworthy manager. My poor computer had to feel my anger when I typed up my résumé in disgust. My poor customers had to learn every minute detail about our product because I didn't want to be anything like that guy. I felt that if the man was shady with his customers and didn't seem to mind the ethics of the way he dealt with them, what was supposed to make me think that he would be honest with me?

**Honesty and integrity are not switches that you can just turn on and off.**

I was his direct subordinate, but I wasn't the only one who felt demoralized by having an untrustworthy manager at the company. The guy who worked in production hated his job because this shady manager made unrealistic promises to customers. The guy who installed the water systems hated his job because when he went to a customer's house he had to deal with angry customers who felt they had been finagled. Thus, one manager's dishonest, aggressive behavior affected everyone, even people who were not his direct subordinates. Ironically, this "improvement" was initiated to help the company, because he was the one responsible for bringing in tons of money and helping the company to "succeed." Instead, it was eating the company apart from the inside out.

In this case, employees were frustrated with the unethical behavior and, more importantly, disconcerted by the implied message that if we wanted to advance in the company we needed to be like Mr. Performance. A peon's hands really feel tied when you realize that you won't be promoted based on your talents or skills, but rather, on your ability to bend the rules and cheat.

How is your management affecting your company? Is your company being eaten apart from the inside out because of you? Are your people going home, boring their spouses, and pounding out résumés because they can't stand being around you?

Mr. or Ms. Manager, look at yourself. Really look at yourself. Remember, you promised you would be honest with yourself. Do your people think you are honest? Now really think about this. Have you ever given them a reason to trust you, or to mistrust you? Does your behavior with your employees, other workers, and customers suggest integrity, or does it reek of dishonesty?

### Do it for the Peon

If this is an area that needs a little work, where do you get started? How do you get your people to trust you? I promised you solutions, right? Well, now I am going to deliver on that promise. See, you can trust me. The first step to becoming more trustworthy is to be dependable, loyal, and steady. Think about the most trustworthy person you know. What is the first character trait that comes to mind when you think of that person? Probably something related to the fact that you know that their behavior will not change. For instance, you could reveal to them extremely confidential information and their behavior remains exactly the same, as if they had never heard it.

Imagine you are about to take a daylong horseback-riding trip, and you are given an option of riding one of two horses. The first horse is an old, reliable horse guaranteed to give you a safe, enjoyable ride with no surprises. The second horse is a bit of a hothead. His behavior is very sporadic. Sometimes he just does what he feels like doing and may take you miles off the beaten trail. Which horse would you choose for the ride? I am going to guess that most people would rather have the steady, trustworthy horse. The most desirable element of that horse's personality is that you can trust it because it is steady and unchanging.

So, the first element of being trustworthy is being steady and unchanging. Okay, that is a good trait over time, but how can you work to gain the trust of your peons today? The best way to gain trust is to do something for someone for which there is no apparent personal reward in return. If you are a direct manager, this could entail something as simple as taking an employee out to lunch or remembering their birthday. If you are an upper-level manager, it could be something as simple (and as complicated) as remembering a peon's name. Trust can be gained by doing things that only benefit the employee.

During the middle and latter part of the 1990s, I—like 99.87% of the U.S. workforce—had visions of making oodles of money through the Internet. I calculated that the ability to design and put together a Web site would be a very valuable job skill. At the time, a friend of my wife's owned a small shop that sold competitive swimsuits. Through conversation with my wife, this friend learned that I aspired to Web design and asked if I would put together a site for her small business. I appreciated her inquiry; however, I had to decline because at that time I did not yet know how to do what she was asking. She responded by giving me an opportunity to learn: "I'll pay you to learn while you make my Web site."

I couldn't believe it. She was going to pay me, by the hour, to learn how to design Web pages, and all I had to do in return was to design hers. It was difficult for cynical old me to figure this out. Sure, she would get a Web site out of the deal, but it would cost twice as much—and probably take ten times longer—to have me rather than a professional do the work.

The thought kept crossing my mind: "Why is she doing this?" I could not come up with a better explanation than "she just wants to help me," with no overwhelming benefit to herself. Once I concluded this about her motives, I can't overstate just how motivated I was to avoid letting her down. I wanted to work twice as hard, to learn quickly, and to make her Web site top-notch. As time went on, she continued to do unselfish things for me, which in turn built up my trust in her.

Trust can be a very valuable asset in your quest to win the hearts of your peons, and you can do many little things that will earn trust. For example, extend the branch of trust and, on days when productivity has obviously become negative rather than positive, let people go home early. It is a small gesture that has no apparent benefit to you, and that can help to build the trust of your peons. Such days might include Christmas Eve or the day before Thanksgiving or some particularly non-productive Friday right before a three-day weekend. Let everybody go early—confuse them by doing something that carries no obvious benefit to you.

What crosses the mind of a peon when you act in this way? At first, we say to ourselves, "What is she gaining from this?" If we can't come up with an obvious answer, then we say to ourselves, "Okay, what does the company gain from this?" If there is still no obvious answer, then our final conclusion is, "Hmm, that is a really nice thing to do. Maybe she really is just a normal person." When others see you as a normal person, they see you as a more trustworthy person. It starts to break down the divide between managers and peons, and the trust gets built as you become a member of the One of Us club.

It has always amazed me that most managers neglect the opportunity to build trust by letting people go early on nonproductive days. Maybe you considered it but felt too afraid of your own boss to lay down a decision. Come on! What happened to all those posters of eagles and fog-covered golf courses with inspirational quotes about "controlling your destiny?" Do you really believe that you control your own destiny? Then act like it. Make the decision.

Really, such a decision should be a no-brainer, particularly in the case of employees in noncritical positions. While I realize company policy may be to only get the actual holiday off, the fact is that if people haven't already taken the day off, they are just coming in to fill their time so that they don't waste another vacation day. Sure, maybe you keep some technical people there to make sure the computers stay running – and a security guard or two – but most people in accounting or marketing or sales come in to the office and get very little done on the day right before a holiday.

**If I'm not working, then what is the difference between not doing it at home and not doing it in your office?**

And don't pat yourself on the back if you let your people go at 4:30 instead of 5:00. I'm talking noon—2:00 P.M. at the latest. Or just give your peons the day off. Don't ask permission from your vice president; you have my permission. This has to be something nice you do for your people, and which has no benefit to you. That is how you build trust: surprise your peons. Make them question your motives. Make them search for a reason behind your actions. Make them come to the conclusion that maybe you are just a normal person. Before long, they will see that you are a normal, trustworthy person who belongs in the One of Us club.

## Communication

Another very important way for you to gain the trust of your employees is through constant, open communication. Don't duck the issue by saying, "Well, I have told them that my door is always open." That is not communication; that's a cop-out. If you want to be a manager that communicates well, understand that communication means clearly explaining everything to your employees, and ensuring that they understand you completely.

**The fact is, if you don't tell them everything, they will make up their own stories, and chances are those stories will be wrong.**

In the absence of any way to discredit them, your employees will believe any fabrication.

For example, imagine two employees are walking down the hall. They see their manager walk into his office with the manager of Human Relations, close the door, and spend over an hour in there. Employees are usually pretty creative. Their minds can come up with any number of explanations for this occurrence. Here are some examples:

- He is having an affair with the lady from HR.
- They are planning mass layoffs and are just checking what they have to do first.
- They are checking to see how many sick days I have taken over the past ten years, because they are looking for a reason to fire me.
- He embezzled a bunch of money and they are on to him. Great! Now my 401k is worthless.

Now, the actual scenario may just be that the manager's wife became pregnant, and he wants to make sure he understands all the benefit plans ahead of time. Nonetheless, a lack of facts will not stop employees from making something up. Until the manager tells them otherwise, they will believe whichever scenario they prefer.

So how does the manager avoid rumors? Obviously, it would be impossible for a manager to explain every action, but managers should try to put themselves in the shoes of their subordinates and to identify which situations might need some explanation. All it may take is mentioning to one team member, "Hey, I was speaking with the HR person today about the upcoming birth of my baby, and our company has some pretty good coverage." Believe me, word will get out.

A manager should strive to communicate everything with employees. Obviously, some things should not be shared, for legal or other reasons, but for the most part, most of the information you currently choose to withhold from your peons could be shared with them without any penalty.

When I worked for a medium-sized Internet company, my direct manager was great about communicating. If somebody from our team left the company or was fired, he brought us all into a meeting immediately. Before we were able to create our own theories about why that person left, he would explain the situation to us from his perspective. This approach was critical to diffusing any negative sentiment toward him or toward other managers. Once we heard his story, we would say to ourselves, "Okay, that makes sense from a business perspective. My job is not in jeopardy for now, so I won't worry about it."

This is quite a contrast with other managers I've worked with, who fire someone, let security escort the former employee out the door, and then lock themselves in their office and wait until everyone leaves so they don't have to confront potential backlash. Had my good manager never taken the time to communicate it to us, our minds would have been filled with wild theories:

- He got fired because he and the manager had that one disagreement.
- She got canned because they are starting to cut back the workforce, and I'm probably next.
- I bet he got fired because he took an extra fifteen minutes on a couple of lunch breaks. I do that once in a while too... I'm dead meat.

This is the way the peon mind works. If you doubt that your subordinates draw conclusions without proper information, watch yourself do the same thing the next time you drive by a rush hour fender bender. As you come up on the mangled autos, you immediately try to create a scenario to explain the different dents and the pieces of glass on the ground. You look at the skid marks, you check to see if you know any of the people involved, and you draw conclusions about what happened and who was at fault.

I know it sounds grotesque, but it's true. Traffic can be delayed thirty extra minutes just because all of us morons have to slow down and create the scenario in our minds. I'm sure that for many traffic incidents, the number of possible scenarios created is the same as the number of cars passing. This isn't unlike peon-contrived scenarios about managers at work. We see an odd scene, we look for clues, we only find a couple of clues—but we come up with a theory anyway.

Sure, it would be nice if your employees would just come up to you and ask. That's what the open door policy is for, right? Unfortunately, that is like going up to someone to tell them they have a booger hanging out of their nose. If the peon doesn't trust you or isn't confident you trust them, they won't bring it up.

Managers, please take the time to communicate to your people about everything. Put yourself in their shoes. Once you get the information, figure out what part they need to know and pass it on to them. Be open with them about everything. It will help you build trust and it will avoid any confusion about your motives.

## Two-faced

Now, don't assume that just remembering somebody's name, giving them a couple hours off, or telling them why another employee got fired will earn their trust for life. As I stated earlier, trust is a funny thing. You must earn it, and you must continue to earn it. More than anything, however, you must do everything in your power to avoid betraying that trust.

So, just how does one betray and lose the trust of others? In my experience, it tends to be the actions that make you appear two-faced that are the most damaging to a bond of trust. What do I mean by two-faced? Exactly what it sounds like: Putting on one face for one person or situation, putting on another face in another situation.

Trust is lost when someone finds that the person they trusted was actually a "face" or a façade. For example, when my wife and I were courting, I successfully convinced her that I was a clean, well-mannered, polite man. Not long after the wedding bands were exchanged, though, I removed that face and showed her the real me—as many people do in marriages. Pretty soon, she was forced to change her own oil, open her own doors, and watch football instead of beauty pageants. Luckily, I am blessed with a wife who was able to see the new face and to trust me just the same. Many employees, however, are never able to work around a manager's betrayal of trust.

How many faces do you have? How many faces do other people see in you? Do you wear the same face for everyone? Do you wear one face for the customer, a different face for the CEO, and yet another for your friends and family? Or are you comfortable with yourself to the point that you can be yourself in all situations, without having to be dishonest or compromise your integrity?

Think about situations where this can come up in the workplace. Imagine a manager who one day tells an employee what a great job they are doing, and states that the employee is right on track for promotion, and then gives that employee a written reprimand for poor work performance a week later. Consider a manager who has no problem rewarding a top performer with plaques, yet is hesitant to recommend that same person for a promotion. Such actions break the bond of trust between not only that peon and the manager but also between the manager and every other peon within earshot, who hears the story of the peon.

Another, subtle example of being two-faced is the manager who fails to follow through on promises or threats. I once worked under a manager who sent all-staff e-mails every Monday, telling us, basically, to double our output and reduce our downtime or find another job. Every Monday. We knew it was coming; it didn't surprise us. Yet nothing ever came of it. By Tuesday, everything he requested or threatened was forgotten, and we went about our business as usual.

We attributed the weekly e-mail ritual to a flexing of management muscle, justifying his position in the company. About all he accomplished, however, was to tear down any trust we may have placed in him. Eventually, we had no confidence in anything the boss said—even to the point that we discredited promises. When he proclaimed pay raises or other benefits, the general feeling was "I'll believe it when I see it."

**How can you truly be a leader if the first reaction to your promises is doubt?**

If you do nothing else after reading this book, strive to earn your employees' trust—but don't expect the level of trust to change overnight. It may take months or years. All people are different, and all people have different personal definitions of trust. If you have already betrayed the trust of the people on your team, work to build it back up, but don't assume it will come back quickly or that you can sweep under the rug the things that you did to betray the trust. You're going to have to work for it.

If you have the trust of your employees, you have everything. Becoming a peon-centered manager will be ten times easier if you first concentrate on establishing a relationship of trust with your employees. All of the other suggestions in this book will only work if they are built on trust. By avoiding the one great personal offense of deceiving someone, you can establish trust between yourself and your peons. Trust is created by performing actions that appear to have no self-benefit, by your constant, effective communication, and by remaining the same person in all situations. By working to become more trustworthy, you will enhance your ability to lead, and increase your peons' desire to follow.

☾

# Get Real

Why do peons work? For the paycheck, right? Beyond the obvious reason that we need money to survive, though, why do we work, and why do we aspire to a larger paycheck? Why do we aspire . . . . .

## Chapter Two

. . . . . **to a more distinguished title** or a better-looking business card, the closer parking spot or the nice big office? Why do we take extra school classes just to get ahead? Why do we do these things?

I realize I'm getting a little philosophical with you, but really, the answer is pretty simple: We work for respect. That paycheck is a message from the world that we are a respectable person. That larger paycheck, and the subsequently larger vehicle we drive is, we feel, a greater manifestation of respect. Most of our reasons for working, and for working hard, can be whittled down to respect.

It is safe to assume, therefore, that if we work for respect, then most motivating factors can be traced back to an employee earning or receiving respect. It is not about a plaque to hang on the wall, and it is not only about the money. If it were, then you would not see high-priced athletes, who are paid plenty of money, demanding trades and opting out of contracts. While the money is nice for them, the fact that some do demand trades and opt out of contracts obviously means it is not everything. Money is only a motivator if it comes coupled with respect.

**The way to truly motivate people is to respect them.**

The plaques, the money, the employee-of-the-month awards—all have to be given in a spirit of respect in order to be effective. Likewise, if I am motivated by respect, whether in monetary or in personal form, then the opposite is also true: My motivation is lessened when I am disrespected.

Disrespect is such a serious offense that rap music has

come up with a shortened version of the word: dis. As in "He be dissin' you girl. Kick him out." Or "Don't dis on my fresh rhymes." Or, my personal favorite, "Ever since he made it big, he be goin' round all frontin' and dissin'."

Since disrespect is a very serious offense, we must establish what behaviors are interpreted as disrespectful and decide how to avoid them. In order to avoid the pitfall of disrespect to peons, and to build the trust toward progress, you must first get real.

When I say, "Get real," I'm talking specifically about adjusting an attitude—the attitude that there exists an imaginary gap between management and peons, and that one is better than the other. Think back to your days in school and to how upset you used to get when some other kid on the playground assumed they were better than you. Remember that feeling of disrespect? All you wanted was to be treated as an equal.

My experience in many workplace environments has been not much different from the playground. In some situations, managers and peons are perceived as completely different types of people. The manager is seen, in his own mind and maybe in the minds of some subordinates, as more educated, wealthier, more successful, and therefore a better person than the lowly peon. In addition, because the manager knows the measly salary of the peon, and knows that she has the power to advance the career of said peon, she may feel a little more power in the relationship. The eyes of the manager look down upon the peon, and the forced eyes of the subordinate look up at the manager.

I realize some companies perform better than others in the area of employee equality. If you work in one of those companies, good for you. However, I am sure there are still areas that need work. So how do you know how well you are doing in the area of employee equality? Don't ask some magazine that ranks you a great place to work—what do they know? When was the last time a magazine writer walked by an executive in the hall without receiving even the courtesy of a "hello"? The writer never has, but the janitor might have experienced this. Therefore, if you want to know how good you are at getting real, go ask your employees. Ask the janitor. Ask the receptionist. Do they get the same rights, benefits, and respect as everyone else?

If you find there is distance between last and first in your company, start addressing that by taking a good look inside yourself. Think about how special you felt when you finally got the promotion to management, or when you first started your business. You probably washed your car that day, or got your hair cut. You started wearing a cell phone or a pager, or maybe both, and had your spouse call you three or four times a day, just to make it look like you had somebody important to talk to. You felt like royalty when they finally put your name and title on the door, didn't you?

And remember the day your new business cards arrived? Oh, that was wonderful, wasn't it? You immediately put twenty of them in your wallet or purse, didn't you? You just couldn't wait to give them out. You found yourself giving them to everyone: the lady at the grocery store, the guy at the oil change place, your dry cleaner. Sometimes you gave them out at places unconventional to business card swapping: at church, at the gym, in the middle of Lamaze class. It didn't matter. You were now a manager, and it served the world right that they should know.

Come on, don't lie. You did that, didn't you? It's all right— you aren't the only one. You loved to go to lunch and see those little bowls where everybody would throw their business cards in hopes of winning a free egg roll. Heck, you'd throw in three or four cards, and you'd make sure that one of yours was sticking face up on the top, so everyone could see your name, with the title under it: *Manager* or *Owner* or *President.*

Take out one of your business cards. Go ahead; I'll wait here. Put down the book and pull one out. Okay, now look at it. It looks good, doesn't it? Does it make you feel powerful? Maybe a little fulfilled, like all your work has paid off. Does it make you feel like somebody special? That's who you are, right? You are J. Doe, Manager, or J. Doe, Owner. That describes you in a nutshell, doesn't it?

Okay, now I want you to do something else with your business card. I want you to put one hand on one side of it and one hand on the other side. Now I want you to tear it—tear it right down the middle. Come on, you sissy, rip it! Do you want me to tell your manager how bad you are at following directions? Rip it with all the aggression you have. Rip it up into tiny, indiscernible pieces.

J. Doe, Manager, is not who you are. You are not your business card, and your business card does not describe you. If it does, if you are one of those people who started to pick up all the little pieces and try to tape them back together again, then you've got it all wrong. That business card, that title, makes you no more of a woman or a man than does an expensive European car, a fancy watch, or a new hair color. If you want your peons to work for you, to trust you, and to respect you, you cannot be J. Doe, Manager, you must be just J. Doe, Person. That is what I am talking about when I say, "Get real."

Thinking back to my time working at a large public company, I recall the illusion of grandeur built up around some senior-level managers. In these situations, many of the lower-level managers, and some of the peons, treated a meeting with a senior-level executive as though they were meeting the pope, and many times that type of treatment went right to the executive's head.

On more than one occasion, we were informed that a senior manager would be coming to our division to come speak to us. We peons were told, "You are so lucky. I worked at this company five years before I ever got to speak with a senior officer." Fabulous. I am giddy with anticipation.

The day before we were to be graced with this visit, word went out that we ought to dress up for the visit. "You should dress for the position you want, not the one you have." So of course, the day of the visit, some people showed up in their nicest Italian suits and department store heels.

Personally, I thought, "This guy has no idea who I am, and he wouldn't give a slick of spoiled milk to know that I am wearing a tie. The fact that I am wearing a tie for this guy will not get me any promotion, any raise, or any bonus. This tie is doing nothing. And to think, I spent fifteen minutes trying to decide whether the yellow tie (which says 'creative and bold') or the red tie (which says 'steady and powerful') would be more impressive."

Some of the lower-level managers acted like reporters at the red carpet of the Academy Awards: "He's here!"

The screech of excitement generated interest among us cube dwellers, and like little prairie dogs, we popped our heads up over the cube walls to see what the commotion was about. "The corporate jet just arrived at the airport. Make sure your desk is clean. Go shine up your shoes one more time."

A person close to the noise signaled back to fellow prairie dogs what was going on, and we all sank back into our holes. Then the screeching started again, and sure enough, the prairie dogs popped up again.

"Okay, they have left the airport, they should be here in fifteen minutes! Are you ready?!"

Play by play, blow by blow, we peons received the action.

"His car is here… and, what's that? Okay, he just opened his door. We have word that the Executive is now stepping out of his car and is on his way in the building. Did you hear that? He's here, he's… What the…? Omigosh! Your tie is on crooked. Hurry! Fix it! For the love of all that is decent in this world, fix your tie!"

The Executive walked into the room, the commotion was too much, and the prairie dogs all popped up to see. The anticipation increased if the Executive was vertically challenged. In such a case, the only thing the prairie dogs could see was a general movement through the crowd, the top of a gray head moving through the masses.

The peons asked themselves, "What does he look like? Is he happy or mad? Did he go with the yellow or the red?"

At some point during the day, everyone herded into a conference area to hear the words of this wise person. Of course, the Executive wasn't already in the room. Oh no! Like a prizefighter, he waited off in the wings, ready to make his grand entrance. The lights came down, the smoke started to pour down, stage lights moving around in all directions—only then would he walk in. There always were some people who stood up, clapped hard enough to do permanent nerve damage to their palms, and started cheering and whistling.

I was amazed at the pompous reception. All these yes-people treating this guy like royalty. Who is he, a prophet of God? The president of the United States, or possibly the author of *The Peon Book*? Heck, is he at least a rock star? No, he's just some vice president of some company. One of the who-knows-how-many thousands of vice presidents of countless companies all over the world. Did he at least cure cancer, further world peace, save some lives? No, he just worked his way up the corporate ladder. He started out as a grocery store bag boy, you know. Then he worked hard and made it to where he is today.

That's nice, but did he get that kind of reception when he was the bag boy? The way some executives are treated, and the kind of applause they get, you'd think they were headed for sainthood. Unfortunately, some executives take the cheering seriously, and they let it go to their heads.

The thing is that, outside of the company, this guy is a normal J. Doe like the rest of us. His card just shows a different title under the name. Does that make him a different kind of person? Does that justify treating this guy like he's someone extremely important? I don't think so. A person outside his company wouldn't think more than two seconds about the choice between yellow and red ties to meet this guy. So this guy is vice president of some company—so what? I was vice president of the glee club at school. What's the big deal?

On my way to work one day, I stopped by a convenience store to fill up on some soda. This was a national chain convenience store, not one of the no-name places that only sell hard liquor, pornography, and stale potato chips. No, this was a high-class corner-store establishment. As I filled my cup with a quality beverage, I saw a bald-headed manager come racing from the back of the store to the front.

"There he is!" he informed his employees. The young kid behind the counter stood there with his mouth open and his shoes untied. Looking around, he saw a lot of people coming in and out.

"Who?" he asked.

"Mr. Whatshisname, the guy in charge of this."

"In charge of what?"

"In charge of all of this, all these stores. You know—one of the bigwigs."

"Oh."

"You better say 'Hi' to him when he walks in."

"I say 'Hi' to everybody."

"I'm just telling you..."

By the time the guy walked in and the kid had complied with the mandatory "Hi," my drink was full and I proceeded to the checkout counter. Mr. Whatshisname was standing there, doing the manager thing and talking to the kid, when I came up to purchase my drink.

I kindly said, "Out of my way, jerk. I'm late for work."

All right, I didn't really say that. Really, I said "Excuse me," the kid took the money for my drink, and I left.

As I drove off, I reflected that this super-turbo manager guy was nobody to me. In fact, he was just another person I could blame for my tardiness. While his presence put the manager on edge and made the peon kid confused, to me, an outsider, this man was just another person. I could very well have called that guy a jerk, or slapped his rear and told him, "Keep it real, baby!" In either case, nothing more would have happened to me than if I did the same thing to an old lady. His business card meant nothing to me, just as yours means nothing to me. I'm glad to hear that you worked hard to get where you are, but this is just a job, it's not who you are.

The point is, most organizations include this imaginary

gap between peons and management, and when you encourage that gap, you disrespect those below the gap. Getting real means not treating your position as manager as some distinguished, elevated chair. Sure, you worked hard to get where you are. Sure, you deserve a little respect because of your position. But you are not Supreme Chancellor, and we are not some lowly, dirty, pond scum peons. We are all members of the human race. We all drive the same freeways to get to work every day. You wait to see that paycheck every two weeks, just as we do. We all go home to families, spouses, kids, and pets. I hate to break it to you, but in the grand scheme of things, we are equals. I know the E-word is a little hard to take sometimes, but it is true.

**Manager = peon.**

In order to maintain a level of respect in the manager-peon relationship, and to narrow the gap, it is important to recognize that we are not your subordinates—we are your co-workers. Most likely, we lack the tenure, experience, education, or abilities that you possess; otherwise, we might have your job and you might be our peon. That is neither good nor bad, it is just part of life. Your position of authority does not make you a better person. It doesn't make you any more important to the company. In fact, as layoffs, rightsizing, fat trimming, and cutbacks show, most companies can live without most management. Companies cannot, however, live without the people who are actually putting the product together and getting the work done.

If manager = peon and peon = manager, then we all ought to act like it. You, as a manager, need to work to break down the imaginary gap where it exists. Work with us as equals. Give us directives as an equal. Announce company policy to us as equals.

Most importantly, when you treat your peons as equals, they will see that they can treat you as an equal. As you come to recognize that your job is as dependent on us as ours is on you, you will see that we really are equal co-workers. There is no room for disrespect when employees view each other as equals. An environment of equality will result in a higher level of motivation than an unequal environment. As peons see that their work is equal in importance to that of the manager, each person will bring a new sense of ownership to their work.

### Empathy

So how do you reach this state of equality? How can *manager* truly equal *peon*? The first step is to strive for another *E*-word: empathy. It amazes me that empathy is such a difficult thing for us to truly show. I guess the reason is that empathy is not something you show at all; it is something you feel.

**By simple definition, *empathy* is the ability to put yourself in someone else's shoes.**

This is different from sympathy, which is to *imagine* what it would be like to be in somebody's shoes. Empathy goes deeper—it is the ability to realistically put yourself in someone else's shoes, because you yourself have worn those shoes.

For instance, I feel empathy when I take my kids to the store and they cry and cry because I won't give them twenty-five cents for a piece of gum. I remember when I was a kid and my mean old dad wouldn't give me twenty-five cents either. I start to actually feel the pain and frustration of being let down by the man who says he loves you. I begin to empathize with my kids. So I give them a quarter, and then all of a sudden they want two quarters so they can get Sticky Piece of Goo instead of the gum. Or they cry because "He got the blue gumball, and I wanted blue. I don't want pink." Before you know it, I spend four dollars in quarters buying gum, until another stupid blue gumball comes out. Then, frustrated, hot, and angry, I injure my jaw on the enormous gum sandwich of discarded pink gumballs in my mouth. At which point I begin to develop a different sense of empathy—for my father.

If you don't have kids, you may have a hard time empathizing with me, but I have a hard time believing that any manager would have difficulty empathizing with their peons. You were all peons once, right? So why do so many managers have such a hard time empathizing with their employees? Why is it so difficult for you to put yourselves in our shoes?

Maybe you do empathize, but you dislike what you see when you get in our shoes, so you elect to spend less time in them. Maybe putting yourself in our shoes makes you realize that a management decision you made was wrong, or a policy you created was a bad move, and you don't want to face that.

Maybe you do put yourself in our shoes, but elect not to act on the impressions you receive while in them. Maybe you remember wearing the shoes, but you don't remember the stinky feet and knee-high tube socks with the blue and yellow stripes that went in them.

I know that when we graduated from high school or college we all thought for sure our first job was going to be vice president of a large corporation; however, after a couple months of job searching, we soon found out that we were qualified only to swim in the shallow end of the peon pool. I have never heard of anybody (other than family) skipping the peon pool and jumping right into the executive hot tub. Even people who start their own business have to go through those first few months or years when they are a nobody, running as hard as they can but getting nowhere.

So how is it that, the minute they are promoted, some people forget what life is like back in the shallow end of our pool? What kind of holier-than-thou training do they give you when you get that promotion to management? Is there some sort of mandatory Management Only meeting, where they put you in a small room with only one light and play a recording of the phrase "You are better because you are management" over and over again, until you believe it?

I realize that it is difficult for some managers to show empathy for employees because they may have come from a different department or a different company altogether. They may have made it to their position without ever performing the exact functions required of their subordinates. But that is not an excuse. The empathy principle can cross over from division to division, from company to company. Your peon shoes may have been Nike and mine are Reebok, but they are both athletic shoes; you can still have empathy for me while watching me walk in my Reeboks.

Don't you remember what it was like to work hard all day, every day, and be paid squat? Don't you remember what it is like to take orders all day from managers that just seemed oblivious? Maybe you still feel that way, but for some reason some of you seem to forget that you were ever a peon, and have a real hard time showing empathy for those under you.

My theory about the apparent lack of empathy is that some managers are insecure or embarrassed about their time in the peon pool. As a peon you may have had bad days, or had months or years in which you didn't perform in the top one percent of the company. You may even feel that this causes current peons to view you as unqualified or unworthy of your post. Your past peon life may strike you as somewhat hypocritical when you preach to us about being mediocre, lazy, or discouraged. I guess these types of managers expect more out of their subordinates than they expected of themselves at that level.

It is important to remember that sometimes there is no way to avoid bad days.

**Peons are humans.**

Until scientists invent an exact peon-replica robot, you are stuck with human peons. You are stuck with people who will have bad days, who will try hard and still not be in the top one percent. You are going to have people who come to work and put in their time but do not aspire to live up to some inspirational words about success. You are going to have people with different motivations and different backgrounds than you. You are going to have people who call in sick when they really aren't ill, or people who surf the Internet at work and minimize the browser real quick when they hear you coming.

You are human too. I am sure some days you aren't going full speed ahead, so recognize the fact that we may have such days too. Rather than expect peon robots, fired up and ready to go every day from the minute they walk in the door, accept the fact that you have human peons. Rather than knee-jerk punishment of an underperformer, why not have more empathy: remember the time when you worked your hardest and still had mediocre results, and try to help that peon work through it the way you did.

Another possible explanation for the lack of manager-peon empathy is the Parent Theory. Managers operating under this theory are similar to overprotective parents—the ones who tell a boy to bring their daughter back by 9:30 P.M., and if she's a minute late, threaten to track her boyfriend down with a shotgun. Most parents like that were probably pretty daring when they were teenagers. Their thoughts go something like, "I know what these kids are doing when they are staying out late. They are doing the same things I did when I was their age…

Oh no they won't!" Such a parent empathizes with their teenager, but only negatively.

Many managers behave the same way. You might have a guilty conscience about the way you slacked when you were a peon (or the way you continue to slack today), and you just know that your people are slacking too, working the system the same way that you always did. This type of manager generally checks up on their employees from the weirdest angles. They know all the best ways to catch somebody slacking, because they thought it all out when they were peons, in order to avoid being caught themselves. This type of manager can be especially dangerous to the average peon because such managers tend to micromanage every minute detail of peon jobs.

**Micromanagement is never an acceptable style of work management.**

I don't know any peon that goes home to their spouse at night and says, "Man, I wish my manager would follow up on more details of my job." If you have to manage every single, minute detail of someone's work, then you might as well do the job yourself.

I don't understand micromanagement as a general practice, and even less as a style of reaction to a business crisis. Too many times micromanagement is used as a "wonder tool" to fix just about any business situation. It never gets the intended results, however, and is only a show of severe disrespect.

To illustrate: Let's say the numbers come in, and your department is way below expected productivity levels. There are a number of different ways you can react. You can analyze the situation and ensure that the peons have the tools to reach that level of productivity (yeah, right!). Or you might analyze your management style, to ensure you are helping your people reach that level of productivity (I don't think so!). Even better, you could reassess the productivity goals to determine if the original goals were unrealistic (yeah, like that is ever going to happen!). While all of these scenarios are acceptable reactions to the problem, they are also the reactions that very seldom occur.

Instead, the low numbers come in and the knee-jerk reaction is to think, "Those peons aren't working hard enough. That's it—enough of the slacking. I am going to get tough." So you walk around with a clipboard and a mission, and you start analyzing every little detail of your peons' work lives: how many breaks we take a day, how many times we go to the restroom (only three bathroom breaks a day, and nothing past 4:30). You analyze what we eat for lunch and how many times we blink in a day, as if managing every sordid detail of a workday is going to somehow change the numbers around. Instead, all you are doing is disrespecting your employees and beginning to alienate them.

This trend will become worse if your micromanagement turns to threats. Maybe you get rid of one of us as a sacrificial lamb, to send a message that four bathroom breaks will not be tolerated: "There is work to do! We are paying you to work. Get your butt behind the desk and work. And until the numbers return to an acceptable level, you are going to have to keep this up."

You might feel a little mean, but that is your job, right? And you continue to manage this way because things start to change. You are happy to go to your boss and inform her that your people have actually limited it to one bathroom break per day, because they go before work, after work, and during lunch. You feel like you are making a difference, and things are turning around. You seem to be rewarded for your micromanagement.

Don't puff your chest out any further, though, because you are not actually getting the results you think you are. The only reason people are taking fewer bathroom breaks is because we are so scared to go we would rather just wet our pants at our desks than risk crossing your path on our way to relieving ourselves. I'm not joking. You have now officially turned yourself into the KGB.

Unfortunately, fear is not an acceptable motivating factor. Fear is no way to run a business. You do what I say or you will be eliminated? If that is your style, then maybe someday you could write a book on all the great management decisions you made in your career and sell millions of copies. You could title it *The Napoleon Book: How to Micromanage*.

Do people enjoy working under those conditions? Does it help them to thrive and be more creative, to take better care of your customers? Do they come to work early because they are excited to be there and they enjoy the work they do? Are they dedicated to your team, and to you, and to working hard to bring the productivity numbers up? Do they feel respected? Absolutely not. All your peons are worried about now is survival. We are petrified of getting on your bad side, so we do what we have to in order to survive, and we wake up every morning hating our jobs. Peons in this situation are certainly feeling no respect or empathy from you.

### Remember

Whether you subscribe to the Parent Theory or to the micromanagement one, an inability to empathize can be a real speed bump on the road to a trusting, personal relationship with your employees. So how are you supposed to show more empathy? I take issue with management books that advocate a particular phrase to indicate empathy, like "I understand" or "I know what you mean," or that rely on gimmicks, such as rephrasing a person's statement, to show empathy.

Instead, in order to show empathy, just mentally put yourself in our shoes. Sometimes this is just a matter of remembering what it's like to be focused on one thing, and then to have management come down and change your direction 180 degrees in one afternoon. Or recalling what it's like to have to ask for time off, or remembering what it's like to be the new guy on the job, having a hard time remembering everything. The overwhelming theme here is that

**empathy = remembering.**

So, if remembering is a skill required for empathy, how

can you develop that skill and likewise develop empathy? Each mind is different, and everyone has different cues that help them recall something. For example, you might put an item on your desk or near your computer, something that reminds you of your first years at the company. Maybe a picture of the company's logo from "back in the day," or a picture of the car you drove when you first started your job. Sure, a picture of your beat-up Mercury is not going to impress people as they walk in your office, but your explanation of why you have it hanging there will.

If you transferred jobs into this management position and you don't have a history with this company, you still might put something on your desk to remind you of your first scrub job. For instance, I could get a model lawn mower, since that's how I got my start, or maybe a model school bus to remind me of the time I drove a school bus to put myself through college. If you work on the road, get a trinket and put it on the dash or hang it from the rearview mirror—a little hammer, if you work construction, or a rubber band, if you manage newspaper deliverers.

Whatever you choose as your cue, get it on your desk today. Look at it often and remind yourself. Put it by your computer, and the next time you get a bad report from someone, or the next time a new person is having trouble understanding everything, look at that bus and remember what it's like to be what the world sees as a nobody. Every time you come up on a job that looks like a four-year-old slopped it together, look at the little hammer or whatever hanging from your rearview mirror, and think about how good it would feel to take that hammer and slam it to the kneecap of the guy that did this crappy job.

Actually, you could take time to look at the hammer and remember what it's like to not know exactly what you are doing, and remember the time when it used to take you ten whacks with the hammer, rather than just two, to drive a in nail.

If you are managing children as a mother or a daycare worker, put a picture on the fridge of yourself when you were a little rug rat. In fact, get a picture of the time your mom caught you playing in her makeup and had the presence of mind to snap a photo—before she sent you to your room for a month and took away your Easy Bake Oven. Put a childhood picture of your husband on the fridge too, so when your boys are acting like they just got back from a field trip to Satan's Lair, you can look at the picture of the cute little boy that ended up being your husband, and you can blame it all on him.

Get real. Respect your co-workers. Keep yourself level-headed. Take time to empathize. Remember to remember. It is not about management versus peons, it is about working together as equals. Take time to put yourself in the dirty, smelly shoes of your peons. And remember that we are all peons in one way or another. If you don't like being treated like a peon, don't treat us like peons either.

☾

# Get Personal

When I began writing this book, I shared it with my mother. She liked the idea, and she told me that in all her leadership positions, people asked her the key to . . . . .

## Chapter Three

. . . . . **being such a good manager.** At first, I didn't hear her advice because I was too busy thinking of my mom as a leader. My mom? Dad was the one structuring billion-dollar deals overseas, not mom. What did she do? This was the woman who stayed at home with eight kids. She wasn't some bigwig in some high-rise building. What management, Mom? The PTA? The church activities committee? How is that management?

Then it hit me, and I realized management doesn't mean wearing a tie or a skirt with a long jacket, or getting special e-mails that you decide either to forward or not to forward. Management is a lot more than a special parking space. It is a lot more than having the power to hire and fire. Management can be found in homes, classrooms, and scout troops. My mom had to be one heck of a leader and manager to handle eight kids without going completely crazy, especially since one of those kids was me. In fact, I'd put my mother's management skills up against those of any CEO managing a Fortune 500 company. Though her résumé looks a lot different, it is not any less impressive—her management skills were just applied in a much different sphere.

Each of us has management responsibilities in some form or another, even if we don't have a special title or a corner office. We might be a parent, a T-ball coach, a dog owner, or the elementary school janitor. In every capacity, however, certain things remain the same, and the advice my mom gave me always applies: Treat people like they are people.

## Treat People Like They Are People

It seems pretty simple, right? But think about that for a minute. Keep thinking about it until the light bulb finally turns on. Take a minute, set the book down, go open the fridge door and just stare into it, or go spend some time in your thinking place. Think about your life, your team, your subordinates. Be completely honest with yourself. Do you treat them like people? Do you know what it means to treat people like they are people?

Here is a million-dollar hint that you are getting for only a couple of bucks: Your peons are not tools for you to use in order to reach your goals, chess pieces in a great corporate game, dishonest little punks that all need firing, cheating slackers that have no internal motivation, or imaginary creatures that disappear when you aren't around. They are people.

I'll bet you are thinking, "I know that. I treat my employees like people. This guy is so stupid." Then you turn over the book and think, "How much did I pay for this? Oh… What a rip-off."

But I want you to be completely honest with yourself. You know, that honest side of you that you rarely even let your family see—just you seriously talking to yourself in the mirror. Can you honestly say that you treat those you manage like people? Like friends? Like family? As you would like to be treated?

Do you know the names of your employees' kids? How about their dogs? Do you know your employees' birthdays, where they grew up, their hobbies, the story of their fifteen minutes of fame? Do you know how your employees met their spouses? Do you know what religion your people practice? Do you really know what makes them tick? If not, why not?

Big deal, right? What difference does it make if you don't treat people like they are people—they all still get a paycheck, don't they? Yes, they do. But when they are merely treated as peons, they are probably gathering the paycheck and doing nothing more. If you showed more interest in your employees personally, they would show more interest in you. When they are more interested in you, they start to do those things that are important to you. When you have given them a gift, such as showing interest in them, they will feel the need to reciprocate that gift. They will give back to you in the form of increased production and better morale while at work.

The opposite is also true. If your people don't feel like you are interested in them personally, then they won't be dedicated to your cause. They will come in and do the work that is necessary to keep their job, but they won't go above and beyond their job description just to help you meet your goals.

It is a reciprocal relationship; in other words, it is a mirror relationship. No matter how much you try, you just can't outsmart that guy on the other side of the mirror. He does everything you do. You raise your arm, so does he. You stick out your tongue, so does he.

**A reciprocating relationship means that your peons' attitude toward you reflects the attitude you exhibit toward them.**

For example, I once worked in a department of a large company where my team was in last place in almost every area of verification. One afternoon my manager asked me to come in to her office, and she said something like, "We are in last place. I don't want to be in last place anymore. What can I do for you, in exchange for your dedication to getting our team off the bottom?"

Apparently, she had asked everybody on the team the same question. I was surprised by her sudden interest in me, so I had her qualify her statement. "What do you mean?"

She replied, "You tell me what I can do to get you one hundred percent focused here at work, and working with me to accomplish this goal."

Her efforts to find out what made me tick surprised me. I was unsure how to react, but I appreciated the attempt to treat me like a person and to realize that I had other motivating factors in my life than just a paycheck. She seemed honest in her personal interest, so I returned her favor with an honest answer, which may have surprised her.

"Honestly, the time schedule is just killing me. Eight-to-five creates all kinds of problems in my personal life. My wife heads to work at 4:30, so I have to get a babysitter for an hour a day, which costs me money. On top of that, it's sometimes a mess to try to schedule, particularly if I have to go anywhere after work: I need her car, because she has the car seats..."

"If I can get you a schedule that would be better for you, will I have your dedication to this project?"

"Absolutely."

"I'm not sure how we can work this. Maybe you can come in early and leave early, or something like that. I'll see what I can get approved."

I'll admit I was blown away. She had shown so much interest in me personally. She didn't come to me and criticize the way I worked or the way I handled things; instead, she asked what it would take to get me to focus. That manager realized that by treating me like a person, and by realizing that I don't disappear into thin air after work, she could get more production out of me. While the issue of the schedule was fairly simple, it was nonetheless very important to me. My happiness after work could be altered 180 degrees just by moving things up an hour.

Now, here is an example of the payoff for treating your peons like people: The next day, I got to work and I was so excited that I worked harder than ever. I also went around to my team members and tried to convince them that the manager was working in our best interest and that we ought to help her out. I was instantly converted to her team, and not only was I working hard for her cause, I was converting others on the team to that cause as well.

Could you use a higher level of dedication from your people? Imagine the benefit of having one or two or six advocates on your team, defending you and your decisions when you aren't around.

**There is a difference in the work ethic of peons when**

**they are committed to a cause, rather than merely completing a task to avoid retribution.**

In order to sway that difference in your favor though, you must treat your peons as human beings.

When you treat your people like people, it will allow them to feel comfortable around you. When they are comfortable around you, they will be honest with you. When they are honest with you, they will tell you how they want to be managed, and you won't have to buy any more management books, because you will be getting it straight from the peon's mouth. And that is what it is all about.

When all is said and done, then, getting personal means getting approachable. When you are approachable, you will find that you are actually working together with your subordinates, like a team. A good manager is part of the team, not just cheering from the sidelines. The employees will bring you on the team when you are personal and approachable.

Are you starting to see the big picture here? Is your frame of mind shifting yet? We are all in this together, we are co-workers; in fact, we are all dependant workers. Get to know your peons and let them get to know you. Be their advocate. Don't be afraid to take off the corporate hat for a few seconds. Be a teammate above all else.

**In fact, be more dedicated to your peons than you are to your own boss.**

Think about that. Your success depends directly on your employees' performance. Your boss may give you a performance review, but your employees are the ones giving you the numbers to take to that review. It makes sense, then, that you should be spending more time developing those relationships than any other ones. It will help your team be more successful because people with whom you have a personal relationship will be committed to your cause. It will also help the peons' morale. When you are personal with them, and they feel like you are their advocate, they will come to you with their concerns, rather than letting such problems fester. When you are not personal or approachable, you can expect the opposite result.

One manifestation of this opposite result is something I call *silent turnover*. It is a damaging kind of turnover where you, as the manager, believe everything is all right with an employee—maybe a few minor problems—and then all of a sudden the employee quits, apparently out of nowhere. In the exit interview, they bring up all kinds of accusations that make you just scratch your head and wonder, who is this person, and what did they do with the real employee?

How does this happen? Did you initially hire the wrong person? Did they have personal problems you could do nothing about? In some cases, it's true, you couldn't have done anything. In most cases of this sort, however, you probably could have done something: You could have been more personal, more trustworthy, more approachable.

Maybe the whole issue started out with a minor concern, but because you were unapproachable you never heard, "I know this sounds crazy, but my dog is really sick, and he is all I have left in this world. I'm having a tough time concentrating today. What do you think I should do?" Instead, the peon called in sick, or took a vacation day and then felt angry that they should unfairly have to burn a vacation day on this.

Maybe you never heard, "I'm really worried about my teenage son—I think he might be taking drugs. I feel this real desire to be home when he gets home from school. Is there some way we can work something out with my schedule?"

The alternative to open, approachable communication is no communication, in which the peons keep everything to themselves. Problems arise, but they never say anything, they are afraid you'll criticize them for having a lack of commitment, or that you might dock them in their next performance review. So, they spend the last two hours of work nervously calling home to see if their son is home yet. Eventually, that employee gets disgruntled because "this stupid company doesn't care about its people." The dissatisfaction then leads to unhappiness, and before you know it, they are sending their résumé to your competitors.

**Turnover is expensive. It looks bad. However, many such scenarios are preventable if someone just shows some personal interest in that employee. The problem isn't that you hired the wrong people; the problem is they don't feel comfortable in the work relationship you have presented to them.**

Getting personal is about creating that environment of comfort for your peons. By being personal with them, and by treating them like people, you will allow them to feel comfortable with you to the point that they bring their concerns to you.

## Make Their Goals Your Goals

So how do you get personal? How do you create that workplace comfort? Well, the answer is a complex formula involving derivatives and difficult four-dimensional modeling…

Actually, it's not that complicated. If you want to get more personal with your peons, first you have to care. That's about it, except for… Nope, that's it. Just care. Stop worrying so much about yourself, and start caring about the lives and well-being of your peons. Change your focus from "How can I get my employees to help me reach my goals" to "How can I help my employees reach their goals (which will in turn help me to reach mine)?"

Remember that your success depends on your peons. Stop hiding in your office. Stop assuming you can't mingle with the peons. Start working with your people rather than against them. Start assisting them instead of telling them. Be proactive in getting to know them. Be interested in them, and they, in turn, will be interested in you. Once you get to know them and to spend time with them, you will see what motivates them and what their goals are. You can then make their goals your goals. Usually, their goals are aligned with yours. Therefore, if you help them to reach their goals, you will indirectly be reaching your own goals. When you focus on the goals of the peons rather than focusing on your own goals, great things will happen. When great things happen, you'll get that promotion—and you will have earned it the right way.

It just takes a change of focus and a desire on your part to be more personal. A real desire. Not because I say so, but because you feel it is part of your job. Because you feel that by performing well in that area, success will come in other areas.

However, it is easy to say, "I'm going to be more personal and interested in them." It is much harder to actually do it. But, since I did say I would give you solutions along with the problems I present, here are some suggestions for getting personal.

One specific area that you could start on today is to set up, by the end of the week, a database that includes the birthdays of the peons directly under your supervision, of their spouses, and of their kids—even if it means getting your assistant to put it together. Remembering these dates when they arrive can be so easy; there are a ton of ways to remember these dates—with a paper calendar, a software program, or even Web sites that will send you an e-mail and remind you that a birthday is coming up.

Another area that you can focus on is to be more attentive to what is important to your peons in the area of, say, pets. Find out what pets your people have, if any. Write them down if you have to, or use the same method for remembering that you use for the birthdays. Just take time and make an effort to really focus on your peons. There are a million areas that you could focus on to get to know them better. One week you could ask them where their ancestors are from. Maybe the following week you can ask everybody the jobs they worked before this one. Every week, come up with a different personal subject that you want to know about your employees, but don't make it some canned question. Don't walk down the aisle of the cube farm and go from cube to cube saying, "Okay, I'm supposed to ask you what kind of music you like." Instead, find time to have conversations with your people. Maybe at lunch, or at the coffee pot, or on the way to the restroom, or when they come into your office to ask a question.

When you start a meeting, for instance, go around the room and ask everyone to give their answer to a specific personal question. Don't do the "tell us something about yourself that nobody knows" bit. That gets real old, real quick. A better approach is to ask everyone on the team what clubs they were involved in through high school or college, or to have everyone tell about the most famous person they ever met. Make up your own questions; the important thing is to look for opportunities to get to know your people better.

## The Naysayers

Now, some naysayers out there may be thinking, "Nay! If I get too personal with my peons, it will dilute my authority, and they will have no respect for me." Some may feel that becoming too personal makes it much more difficult when you have to enforce the rules with your team. To those naysayers, I respond, "Nay! If handled correctly, the manager who maintains personal relationships with peons can actually do a better job of handing down the tough sentence, without losing any authority."

To illustrate, let's look at a situation where a manager has created a personal connection with her employees, and the employees think that is the green light to freedom. Some employees may say, "Oh, I'm not worried about Jane. She's cool; she won't care if I take off today at two o'clock and go to the game."

This does not mean that Jane has lost control of her workers, that the employees don't respect her, or that she is not an effective manager. It simply means that the employees are comfortable with Jane, that they trust her, and that they know that she cares about them personally. This employee assumes Jane will see the act of leaving work early to go to a ball game as a necessity that supersedes the need to work—which is the way the employee sees it.

Does this mean Jane has to see the situation the way the peons do? Will she betray their trust if she doesn't see it that way? Does that mean Jane can't lay down the law when changes need to be made? Once again, the answer is no. In fact, the peon-centered manager probably will have more success at discipline, because a peon-centered manager has established a relationship of equality rather than of hierarchy.

When you treat your employees as equals, and you recognize the personal elements of their lives, they will do the same. They will recognize and be respectful of the fact that enforcing company policy is part of your job. If done properly, a potentially negative situation can actually turn positive, helping to build a more personal relationship between the peon and the manager. Your peon can actually come out of the situation with increased trust in and respect for you. However, you must concentrate on maintaining the personal concern for them while also having the courage to be strong and lay it on the line.

As you go into a policy-type situation, trust in your friendship with that employee, and trust in the personal relationship you have developed. Trust that the equal respect you have established enables you to give feedback without fear of damaging the relationship—just as only a true friend will tell you when your breath stinks. (By the way, your breath stinks.) In a truly mutually beneficial relationship, you shouldn't worry about rejection from the other party—

**just make sure that when enforcing policy, you still treat people like they are people.**

They are still co-workers and friends, they still have families, etc. You just need them to change a behavior.

Jane, for example, can approach her policy-enforcing situation in one of two ways. The first way is to focus less on the employee and more on herself. She may pull Dave into her office and say, "Dave, you left work early yesterday. Somebody told me he saw you at the baseball game, on the TV highlights. That is unacceptable behavior. We need employees with more commitment. If you aren't going to be committed to this company, then maybe you don't belong here. I am going to take those three hours out of your next paycheck, and I don't want to see this happen ever again, or you will be facing a written reprimand and possible termination."

This approach leaves Dave thinking, "Jeez. What a jerk. She was all cool yesterday, and now this. (I don't trust her anymore.) It was three freaking hours—why is she making such a big deal? I saw her leave early the other day…"

A better way to approach the situation would be for Jane to bring Dave into her office and say, "Dave, I didn't see you yesterday afternoon. What happened?"

Because Dave trusts Jane, he levels with her. "Actually, I went to the game."

"The Diamondbacks game? Really?"

"Yeah, it was great! We won—seven to four."

"Did anybody from work see you there?"

"Yeah, I got hit by a bat in the forehead 'cause I was dancing and wasn't paying attention to the game. It was on the news last night."

"No way! On the news? That's rough. How many beers did you have?"

"None. It's just that disco music. They start playing 'Play that Funky Music' and I just can't stay in my seat. You'd be surprised how few places there are to duck when everything mysteriously slows down and all you can see is a baseball bat flying at your forehead. I felt like a bug getting sucked into one of those bug zappers! I knew what it was, I knew the damage it could do, yet I just kind of watched it move through the air toward me until it smacked me right in the noggin."

"Oh my gosh! Are you okay?"

"Yeah. But no more of these seats close to the dugout. From now on, the only nosebleeds I'll be getting will be from the altitude of the seats."

"So you skipped work to go to a baseball game and you got hit in the face with a bat. That ought to tell you something." Jane laughs.

"Yeah, you're right." Dave laughs too, rubbing the tender spot on his head.

"I didn't get a request for time off," says Jane. "Did you forget to send that?"

"Aw, actually, I, uh, I was just thinking that you'd be cool, just kind of overlook it."

"Well, Dave, I wish I could. But if it weren't a big deal, I would have gone to the game too. You can't just take off the afternoon like that, while everybody else is working, and expect to not use vacation time."

"Aw, c'mon Jane. Tell you what: I got to keep the bat that whacked me; I'll give it to you. I'll even clean off the blood. I just don't want to waste any vacation time on this one. I only have two days left of vacation, and with the holidays coming up and all…"

"Sorry, Dave. I wish I could help you, but you know how vacation time works."

"Yeah…" Dave's face sinks, realizing that the jig is up.

"So the time-off request?"

"I'll send you a request for some vacation time. You'll get it this afternoon."

In this second example, Jane was able to still enforce the rules, without being a jerk about it. Dave knew that what he did was against the rules; he knew he didn't have permission to go to the game. The thrill of hooky was part of the fun. He hoped that Jane would overlook it, but realistically, he probably wasn't too surprised that he had to use some vacation time. He was just trying to get away with it. Jane was able to enforce the rules, establish a good precedent for similar instances in the future, and she didn't damage the personal relationship in the process.

The biggest difference between the first example and the second, though, is that in the second case Dave leaves Jane's office thinking, "I wonder how much I could get for that bat on eBay." His opinion of Jane hasn't changed at all; he understands Jane's job and her responsibilities. He hoped that she would be a slacker like him and forget her responsibilities, but it's not very surprising that she didn't, and he doesn't hold it against her. In fact,

**Jane's reaction will earn her Dave's respect because she handled the situation with respect for him.**

She asked him—rather than telling him—to be responsible for his actions.

When peons do stupid things like going to the ballgame, we know exactly what we are doing. We weigh the options and we take a calculated risk. We put our hand out to verify that the wall we've been told is marking the boundary is, in fact, actually there.

**The management response to peons testing the boundaries doesn't have to be one of dominance and severe punishment. Rather, it can merely consist of an acknowledgment that the boundary was tested, and a verification that it is there.**

When handled with respect for the peon, the situation can be a learning experience for the employee, as well as an opportunity for the manager to receive additional respect from the employee. When peons are treated like people, they will reciprocate, and when they respect their manager, they will work to help their manager accomplish his or her goals. When you make their goals your goals, they, in return, will make your goals their goals.

Good managers are not necessarily the ones who have a motivational quote for every meeting. They are not always the ones who are the first into the office and the last to leave, or the ones who never take lunch. Effective managers are not the ones with a smile plastered on their face, nor are they necessarily the ones who were great performers back when they were peons. They are not managers who read all the management books and become certified through training courses. Effective managers are the ones who get personal, recognizing the personal elements of their employee's lives. They are the ones who treat their people like people and who go out of their way to help the employees reach their individual goals, knowing that in return the employees will help out with the management goals.

## Treat People Like You Are People

The follow-up to treating people like people is the somewhat obvious "treat other people like you are people." In other words, come to grips with the fact that you are human too. Don't be the manager that makes the grand entrance to a meeting. Don't expect people to wear red ties and bright red lipstick every time they gather to hear you speak. Resist being the type of personality that makes a kid nervous to greet you when you walk into his convenience store. Don't take yourself so seriously.

**You also shouldn't be ashamed of the fact that you aren't perfect.**

The person that hired you for your management position hired you the way you are, imperfections and all. Why should you feel the need to change who you are to fit the Manager mold? I once read a statement by Judy Garland: "Always be a first-rate version of yourself, instead of a second-rate version of somebody else." Recognize the fact that you are a normal person and that you hope others expect nothing more out of you than that. Don't try to be some model of perfection that just isn't who you are.

You are human, you make mistakes, you aren't perfect. So what? While it is noble to strive for perfection, don't try to convince yourself that you are already there. Don't try to convince your peons that you are perfect, either, because they won't believe it. Even worse, they will look for flaws and try to disprove you. People are smart—even the dumb ones.

I have seen this pattern when I talk to kids. Sometimes, for fun, I will tell them that I am the smartest man alive. Without fail, every time I tell them that I know everything, their immediate rebuttal is, "Okay, what is infinity plus infinity?" or some other question that they think I would never know. Is the problem that I don't look like the smartest man alive? No, the problem is that all of us inherently expect other people to prove their claims of perfection.

So how do you show your peons you are a normal person? An attitude readjustment is the first step: focus on being yourself in all situations. Take a second to step outside yourself and to analyze how you act around different audiences. Do you change? Of course you do, we all do. But focus on your different personalities. Are you a totally different person around your boss than you are around your peons? In order to really have a strong, personal, trusting relationship with your peons, you must have very little variance in your personality. They must trust you to be the same loyal manager, even when you are behind closed doors with your boss. Also, pay attention to your response to personal questions, and analyze those answers to determine if you are really treating your peons as though you are human. Here are some examples.

Question 1: How did you get promoted to this job?
Answer 1: I established goals nobody had ever accom-

plished before, worked ten more hours per week than anybody else, and I accomplished those goals.

This answer is bad. You may have done these things, but when you tell someone this, their thoughts will include the words *corporate geek* and *liar*, and they'll probably be thinking, "I would never do that." In other words, you'll inspire no one but yourself.

Answer 2: Well, in my last position, I was blessed with a great assignment, a fun team to work with, and a little bit of luck. We got along so well; it was like all pistons were firing perfectly. My boss liked what she saw, so she recommended me for this position, and I guess I got a little lucky.

This answer is better. Sure, you worked hard, and we all know the harder you work, the luckier you get. When you admit you've had some luck, it makes you much more likable.

Question 2: What are your plans this weekend?

Answer 1: Well, I'll be staying late tonight, and I'll probably come in tomorrow to work on fine tuning the XYZ project. Then I'll spend Sunday getting ready for that Monday meeting.

This answer is bad, first, because if this is truthfully what your weekend holds, then you need to get a life. Second, even if you are planning to work over the weekend, make it sound more real—tone it down a bit. Working that much won't impress anyone, but you will make people feel uncomfortable if you tell them you are going to put in twenty hours of work on a weekend.

Answer 2: I'm just going to relax this weekend. I'll probably stop in here to fix up the XYZ project and spend a little time on the Monday meeting. I know for sure I am going to set aside some time to take a nap!

This answer is better. Oh yeah — the lovely weekend nap. Everybody loves their nap, and when I find out you love your naps as much as me, I'll accept you into the One of Us club.

I have had experience with managers who were very reluctant to reveal personal information about their kids, about where they were from, about stuff they liked to do away from work, all under the guise of professionalism. The perfect image made us suspicious, however, and we peons all tried to get whatever dirt we could on those managers. Frankly, we didn't trust them. If they were unwilling to trust us with personal information, why should we trust them about other things, such as honest feedback or new innovations? How could we be sure they would handle it correctly?

Remember the mirror? The way you act and treat your employees will determine how they, in turn, treat you. Once managers start to reveal themselves and admit they are human, that they have feelings too and aren't just corporate robots, peons will not ridicule them or lose respect for them. Rather, because of their imperfections, we peons accept them into our One of Us club, and things run smoother after that.

Once you have accepted the fact that you are human, and you are able to open up to your peons on a personal level, you still may have some things to work on in order to truly treat people like you are people. For example, how do you handle vacation or sick time? For some reason, many managers are afraid to use their vacation or sick time. While it is noble to want to work through illnesses, please, if you are sick, don't come into the office. The last thing you want is a team full of sick people. Get yourself healthy and then come in. Similarly, vacation time is yours, so take it. I have seen managers fail to use their vacation time, or wait until they absolutely had to take it—and then spend half their time in the office anyway.

Some managers approach vacation time as if it is some sort of required nuisance. I don't understand this at all. Is your work that much a part of your life that you can't afford to live without it for a couple of stinking days? What are you, some kind of work addict? Just can't wait for your next hit of corporate mandates? Or maybe you are convinced that as a manager, you make that much of a difference at work, that the cost of your absence is too high to justify being out a day.

While you are an important element of the job, the job certainly can be done without you there. Go ahead; we can take care of ourselves. In fact, at some of my previous jobs, our teams were actually more productive when the manager was out. Who knows, maybe it is that way at your work. Try it. Take a week off, and see how much more productive your people can be in your absence. Realize that they will be able to get the work done without you there.

Vacation time is given to you to take, so take it. And when you are on vacation, go on vacation. Even if you spend the entire time at home, don't turn on your laptop. Don't check your e-mail, don't check your voice mail, turn off your cell phone. Vacation time is provided to you as a way to relieve the stress of day-to-day work and to allow you a chance to recharge your batteries and return refreshed, renewed, and ready once more.

If you don't take a real vacation or otherwise take advantage of that time by eliminating all work behavior, you actually do a disservice to your employees and to your company. Believe it or not, the company wants you to take vacations; it is a win-win situation. I'm sure the company would rather have a recharged manager full of ideas and full of energy than one who has been chugging away, day in and day out, yet is a little dry and worn out. I understand that some industries must limit vacation times during the busiest seasons. But at other times, use your vacation time—it'll do you good, and it will help you and your peons to establish a more personal relationship, realizing that both parties are just normal people.

I hate to break it to some of you, but there are more important things in life than your job. Vacation time allows us all to find the balance between work and the rest of our lives. Here is another million-dollar question for only a couple of bucks: Where does work fall on your list of priorities? If it's at the top, then you screwed up, and you are getting life all wrong. There is much more to life than work.

If you don't get my point, think about the events of September 11, 2001. That day should have made all of us realize that we are just normal people. On that day, how concerned were you about your job? All of a sudden, where did work fall on your list of priorities? Hopefully, it fell to around number three or number four. That day, as I sat at my cube and nervously scoured Internet news sites for an explanation of the horror, I realized that I had absolutely no desire to be sitting at work. My paycheck didn't matter so much anymore. All of a sudden, my life's priorities were all lined up, and work was definitely not at the top. I am sure that your experience was similar: You realized that there was so much more to life than work, and work was finally put where it should be on your priority list.

Now, don't interpret this the wrong way. I am not saying it is wrong to strive for success. I am not saying it is wrong to work hard or that work shouldn't play an important part in your life. I'm not saying that it is easy to get away from the office. All I am saying is that you must make sure that your priorities are in the right order, and you accomplish that by keeping a balance between work and life. You do it by using vacation time to focus on the things most important and by treating your peons like you and they are all, simply, people.

So, take your vacation time. Take your birthday off. Take off to go limbo on the beach. Take off for no reason at all. Don't pass up a free opportunity to spend time with your loved ones, whether that means spending time with your spouse, kids, sibling, cousin, parent, or grandparent. Or, you can take your vacation time and just spend time alone relaxing, recharging your batteries. Offering vacation time is not just a necessary evil put in place to keep peons working at your company. It is a wonderful opportunity to help you be a better person, a better worker, and a better manager.

Get personal. Treat people like they are human beings, and acknowledge that you are a human being too. Use your vacation time to get back in touch with your human self. Realize that everyone, including you, has faults and weaknesses, and that we all make mistakes. Take time to focus on helping your peons reach their goals. When you help them reach their goals, they will reciprocate. And when you are faced with the managerial task of enforcing rules, don't punish a peon for making mistakes, but to work with them to eliminate such mistakes from their behavior. Recognize that it is not management versus peons; instead, we are all in this together.

# Get in the Trenches

My father wanted his boys to learn how to work. We used to tell people that Dad was the kind of guy who would have us dig a hole, just to have us fill it back in. We lived in a . . . . .

## Chapter Four

. . . . . **modest neighborhood** where animals such as horses, cows, and chickens were kept in the backyard. Because we had animals, there was always an array of chores my father could assign to my brother and me, to teach us his feared Work Lessons. We enjoyed the "privilege" of doing everything from cleaning up the chicken pen floor to digging a hole big enough to bury a dead cow.

One particular Saturday, for instance, my father had us tear down the wire fence we had around our chickens and put up a seven-foot brick wall. A brick wall around a chicken coop! Now, think about that for a second. What weirdo builds a brick wall around chickens? Is the wire just not strong enough for these brutal animals—you have to put up a concrete-fortified brick wall? What are they going to do, ram the fence and topple it over? They're chickens! I never did get a reasonable explanation about why we built that fence.

My father was a businessman during the week, but on Saturday he worked. He woke my brother and me up at 6:00 A.M., and every Saturday he said the same thing: "Get up! We've got work to do." Oh, those dreaded words. I would lie in bed and act as if I hadn't heard them. I cursed my brother when he got up and started getting dressed. "Get back in bed, you idiot," I whispered. "Just act like you didn't hear him."

Some of those Saturdays were brutal, but all those Saturdays taught me a lesson. While the work was hard and my motivation was lacking, my father showed me a true trait of leadership: He led.

**His wake-up call was always the same, and it always included the word we.**

My father was not as young and durable as we were, yet he always seemed to work harder than we did. He showed us how he expected to get the work done, and his own work ethic always set the tone for our intensity in work. He never asked us to do any work that he wasn't willing to do himself. My father led by example; he led by spending time in the trenches.

My father's example is a powerful lesson in management. **A manager should spend time doing the job he is asking his peons to do** —and not just for a couple of minutes. You should spend a significant amount of your time performing the job functions of your peons, rather than just watching peons and then analyzing their work. Flip a few burgers, pack a few groceries, pick up the phone and answer some customer-service calls, go out and make a sale. You should have a working knowledge of your peons' jobs beyond the knowledge you gained when you did the job ten years ago. Change is the only constant in business, and their job has changed since you did it. So roll up your sleeves and get back in the trenches. How can you possibly expect your peons to respect your opinion and coaching if you've never actually done the job yourself?

I once took a tour of a package delivery facility at an airport. The manager leading the tour told us that he spent many hours out moving boxes and crates with the rest of the workers. However, when our tour made its way to where the peon element was located (that is, where the actual work was performed), it was apparent that he did not do any such thing. I observed the employees watching and chuckling (away from the manager's view) as he tried to operate a crane-like device and failed miserably. I could tell by the expressions on the employees' faces that it had been a long time since they had seen him work the crane, other than in theory. This manager lost some of the respect of his employees that day, and subsequently, some of his power as their manager, because of his inability to perform this elemental function of their job. Had he spent more time in the trenches, rather than up in his air-conditioned office, he would have been a much more effective manager.

Spending time in the trenches allows you to develop a more personal relationship with your employees, and it creates a more trustworthy manager. Imagine that you are one of those workers at that loading facility. Let's say, too, that your manager is not like the one I saw, and instead is always out there working with you, taking turns operating the crane. When he then comes up to you and asks you to operate the crane a little faster, you can respect his advice. He understands what it means to ask you to work it faster, because he has done the job himself.

### "I'd like to see you do this."

The converse is also true: Put yourself in the place of those employees I saw, who have a manager that is the type who sits in his office all day and has never been seen working the crane. That same manager then comes to you and says you need to work the crane faster. The first thing that will come out of your mouth the minute he leaves will be, "Oh, he makes it sound like it's so easy to just speed it up. What does he know? Has he ever even worked a crane? I don't think so. I'd like to see him get out here and do it."

You've said that before, haven't you? We all have. "I'd like to see you do this." How many times have your peons said that about some mandate you have given them? I know some of you think that once you leave they get all motivated and get right to work. I hate to burst your bubble, but usually that isn't the case. I'm guessing that in a lot of cases their response is more along the lines of "I'd like to see him/her do this."

In fact, that phrase is probably the most popular phrase around water coolers, coffee pots, and copy machines around the world. At all the companies where I've worked, and at all the watercoolers I've stood around, that phrase is definitely the one most repeated. It may be spoken in different languages, in different tones, at different businesses, but the consensus is the same: we'd like to see you do it.

The overwhelmingly common use of that phrase is an indication of our frustration with the general out-of-the-trenches style embraced by most managers. If that's the feedback, then, use it. You are getting an undercover view of what really goes on behind your back, and the consensus is the peons would like to see you do their job.

No peon in his right mind would come up to you and say this, of course. The fear of subsequent downsizing is too great. But here I am, telling you, so do something with it. Get in the trenches, get doing the job. Don't just preach about it—do it!

The misconception here for many managers is that they have to be the best at performing the function, or that they have to set the standard. If the normal loading time for that crane operator is twelve minutes, and the manager is asking the peon to do it in eleven minutes fifty seconds, he doesn't have to get out there and do it in eleven minutes flat. The manager only needs to be able to perform the function well enough to show that he understands the goal is hard, but also feels that it is reachable. Employees will believe in the goal a little more if they first believe the boss knows what he's talking about.

The message received by the employees then goes from "Do what I say, and not what I do" to "Look, I know it's tough to get it loaded in twelve minutes. Heck, I couldn't do it. But I know that you are one of the most skilled workers we have, and I am confident you can do it under twelve." What was previously a huge de-motivator, the unwanted raising of goals, has now become a motivator. This is not because of what you said or because you used some catchphrase, but because you have spent time in the trenches. That experience allows you to give truly constructive criticism.

Over the years, I have been the recipient of bad management from managers that did not spend time in the trenches, but one in particular takes the cake. It was a great "how not to" example, provided not by a boss but by my high school principal. I went to a large high school (between 2,500 and 3,000 students) in Mesa, Arizona. Our school was very competitive in all sports, but particularly in football. During my senior year, we struggled through a tough season, but we turned it on in the playoffs and made it to the state championship.

I played on that team, and of all my responsibilities (player hydration, mascot duties, equipment manager), my favorite was the kickoff team. It wasn't the most glorified assignment on the team—people in the stands rarely noticed you—but it was the most fun. I know of no other legal sport where you run full speed at someone and try to hit him so hard that his teeth are implanted firmly in the back of his own neck. Nevertheless, as part of the kickoff team, our job was to run real hard and clobber somebody on the other team.

My responsibility was to contain the runner. When our team kicked off the ball, I lined up on the left side of the kicker, all the way over toward the sidelines, to make sure the guy who caught the ball didn't get outside of me and run right up the sideline. For some reason, once a football player starts running up the sideline, some superhuman booster kicks in and they suddenly become ten times faster than they were in the middle of the field. It was my job, therefore, to make sure that didn't happen. The assignment generally came with very little fanfare. I almost never got to run-and-clobber because I was always waiting to make sure the guy didn't try to sneak up the sideline.

The coin toss at the beginning of the state championship game determined that we were going to kick off first. We all lined up in our positions, and as our kicker got his little football stand ready and tried to balance the ball on it, I started to notice the fans at Arizona State University stadium. I calculated that there were 40,000 of them, and by my calculations, that meant that there were at least 5,000 eligible ladies in the stands watching me. That got me pretty excited. This was my chance to really make a statement and show the girls of the world that they were seriously undervaluing my stock. If I was going to make that kind of statement, though, I needed to do something spectacular. I needed to be the hero. I needed to steal the show. So I came up with a foolproof plan.

The plan consisted of me outrunning the other guys on our kickoff team, weaving through the blockers, and hitting the guy with the ball so hard his helmet popped off. Yeah, that's it. Then, the ball would come flying loose and I'd have the presence of mind to pick it up and run it back into our end zone, starting the game off in amazing fashion. After scoring the touchdown three seconds into the game, I'd go back to the sidelines with my helmet off, pointing and winking at every pretty girl in the stands. Oh, it was perfect. And to top it all off, the other team would be totally demoralized and they would never recover, thus ensuring my team's victory. I decided that would be a glorious, spectacular way to start the game. It would get my name in the newspaper, and it would definitely get me at least ten percent of the phone numbers of those

5,000 eligible ladies in the stands—even a few phone numbers of girls from the other school.

I was pumped. I was ready to make an impact. Soon, the referee blew his whistle. Our kicker raised his hand, trotted up, and booted the ball. My team took off running, building up speed while our opponents ran back and prepared a blocking wall. As we got closer to the human wall, the guy who caught the kickoff started running toward us. Just then, he broke to his right, which meant he was coming right at me.

This was it; it was all falling into my plan. I was at full speed, he was coming at me—the next step would be the helmet rolling on the ground. I could see the headline in tomorrow's paper: "High School Team Wins State, Thanks to Haynes." I could imagine all the girls cheering.

I started to crouch down, to get ready to hit him, but he apparently didn't see the same dream as me. He juked one way and then ran the other, and before I knew it I was reaching out in a lame attempt to trip him as he ran by me. My legs fell out from under me as my left hand grazed his thigh. He ran to my left, which meant, since I was the last guy on the left, he now had a clear path down the sideline.

I tried to disappear as I watched him run another twenty or thirty yards before somebody (I believe it was our team's kicker) finally tripped him up. I slowly pulled myself up and started to jog back to our sideline.

"Maybe nobody noticed," I thought. "I mean, I know my job is to contain, but Coach will be happy that I was so aggressive. Maybe Coach will blame somebody else. If he says anything, I'll just blame the kicker." The floodgate of justifications was open, and I was taking any one I could find.

As soon as I had convinced myself that everything was okay, however, I got close enough to see Coach's face. It was obvious that he did see the play and knew exactly who was to blame. I don't remember everything he said to me when I got off the field, but I'm sure it included the words *contain, you have one job*, and *disgrace*—peppered with a number of four-letter words. I just stood there and took the ranting, raving, and spitting, and even though I felt like a bag of dirt with glasses, I felt he was justified. I did screw up. I did only have one job to do, and my failure to do it had cost us dearly.

After the head coach provided me with colorful feedback, one of the assistant coaches felt he needed to add to what was already said. His criticism sounded somewhat similar, except he had a higher voice and wasn't as loud. I felt he too was justified, so I stood there taking the verbal punishment, hoping it would soon end.

I say that I felt like they were justified because these were men who were out on the field at every practice, going through the drills with us, working with us face to face, down in the trenches with us. They had told me time and time again what my responsibilities were. They showed me how to do it, but I had chosen to ignore that.

After getting a double dose of the feedback medicine, I felt pretty much like a kid that got first place in a Stupid contest. I slipped back through the other players on the sidelines and found a lonely spot to stand, over by the thirty-five-yard line. I just stood there by myself, vaguely watching the game, trying to get back to my "I am Superman" dream. But it wasn't as happy any more. No hit, no fumble, no score. Worst of all, no ladies. As I stood there, I started to reason with myself once again.

"I don't think any of those 5,000 girls saw that. Yeah, that's it. They were probably up there talking with their friends. Yeah. And even if they were watching, they would have no idea what *contain* is. And even if they did, they wouldn't be aware enough to notice that I screwed it up. Yeah, that's it. For all I know, they saw my feeble dive at the guy's legs as a noble attempt. Yeah, those girls in the stands think I am a hero. I bet they are staring at my rear in these tight pants right now. Take a good look, ladies. The Dave Show is in full effect."

As I stood there with a defiant smile on my face, visualizing my success with the ladies, I didn't notice someone invading my sulking space. It was our high school principal. He was a short, old man who was preparing for a nice relaxing retirement after that school year. I am sure this principal occupied a pretty distinguished position. He was principal at one of the most successful schools in one of the most successful districts in the state. He even had his PhD. He had been at that school for a long time, and his teachers and colleagues respected him. But I, a lowly student, did not know him. I'm sure he was too busy to get to know all the students. In fact, I don't think I'd ever seen him at our school except for a few assemblies now and then. To me, he was just another old guy with a bad hairpiece.

Anyway, as I was standing there figuring that my stock in the ladies market was still doing okay, the principal came over to me and yelled, "What were you thinking? You need to contain, damn it! You let that guy get all the way to the forty! Pay attention!"

I turned to see who was yelling at me. This little man in his suit was all upset, his hairpiece was in a tizzy. For some reason, he thought that because he had some authority over me as a principal, he had all authority over me. However, his authority over me as a student did not carry over to the football field. Here was a man yelling at me who had never been outside to offer advice on a hot Arizona afternoon during practice. Here was a man who had never established himself as a football authority to me. Here was a man who didn't even know my name, offering me his "expert" advice on how to play football.

While I felt that the other razzings were justified, I just looked at the principal, amazed that he had the guts to tell me what to do. Who did he think he was? I respected the other coaches. They had been in the trenches with me and had earned my trust as experts in the field. But this principal, no matter how many PhDs he had or how much money he made or how respected he was by district officials, had no more authority to tell me what to do than the water boy did. I became very angry that this dislocated superior felt that he could offer his advice.

So I looked him in the eye, shook my head, and with all the eloquence of a teenager I said, "Whatever, dude." Then I walked away.

Obviously, this principal would have failed Dave's management class. He spent no time in the trenches but still expected me to care about his opinion. If you want your people to respect your opinion and listen to your suggestions, then you have to spend time with them on the front lines. Otherwise, whenever you give advice they are going to be thinking, "Who does he think he is?"

**It doesn't seem possible to effectively coach somebody on how to flip a burger or drive a school bus or write some new code if you've never done it yourself.**

Oh sure, you read the employee training manuals, but does that make you qualified to give relevant criticism?

For example, let's say you don't know how to swim, so you come to the Peon School of Aquatic Competence, where I'm a teacher. On the first day, I stand on the deck and tell you to jump in and move your arms in circles—and, oh yeah, don't forget to kick your legs. I assure you that will get you to the other side of the pool. When you inquire of me, though, you realize that I don't actually know how to swim myself; I just watch people swim all day long, and it doesn't seem like it would be that difficult. I mean, I do have a master's degree in swimming administration, and I have read all the latest training literature. The simple fact that I have never done what I am asking you to do shouldn't make that much difference, right?

That example seems a little ridiculous, but no more ridiculous than managing without spending time in the trenches. Just as my school principal was not justified in coaching me in football, you are not justified in coaching your peons if you don't do their work on a regular basis. Not just once or twice while saying, "See, this is how you do it." I'm talking get in the trenches. Get dirty; do the work.

Do you have any idea what your peons do day in and day out? Really? Have you ever spent a day trying to do their job? Do you know how to perform their job? Do you even know what they do? Do your people see you in the trenches during the day, working, rather than just monitoring or coaching them, or do they just see you at the beginning of the day and the end of the day, verifying that they are present? Are you the kind of boss that rolls up her sleeves and gets involved with the work, or the kind that just watches and assumes her perch up in the clean air of Management? Walking around all day monitoring your people, making sure they do their job, doesn't count. That is not being in the trenches; that is standing at the side of the trench, watching. What I'm talking about is actually picking up a shovel and digging.

Instead, are you sitting up in your office reading management books when you should be down on the floor working? Are you basing your managerial decisions on mere theory or on experience? Put the books down, put the theories away, stop going to two-day conferences that promise to make you a "dynamic, twenty-first-century manager." Get on the floor and lead by example: *We* have got work to do.

Leading without spending time in the trenches can be dangerous. To illustrate this, let's say you are the manager of a fast-food restaurant. The owner notices his profits dwindling and he pulls you in to a meeting to tell you that it is your responsibility to turn this restaurant around. He says you need more revenue, more profit, and higher customer satisfaction.

So, you go back to your fast-food employees and tell them they need to sell more combo meals. This will bring in higher revenue and higher profits, and the customers will be happy. But wait a minute. Let's say you actually spend time at the counter taking orders and serving food. You notice a lot of people coming in, buying a ninety-nine–cent cheeseburger, counting out the change, and leaving. You try everything you can to sell them a combo meal, but they don't buy it.

You start thinking about it, and you remember hearing that the economy is in a slump, or you recall that a large production facility down the street is going out of business, or whatever. Eventually, you realize that people are not coming to your restaurant for the great food and fast service; they come because they can appease their hunger at a relatively low cost. Using that knowledge, then, you can change your focus and still make more revenue and more profits. Moreover, because you are catering to the customer, you will keep satisfaction high.

How would you draw such conclusions about your consumer without actually spending time with them? Certainly, it is possible that your subordinates will tell you what they see. It is possible that you could draw a conclusion about the economy or the production plant without talking to actual customers. But it is also possible that you wouldn't. You then might get upset with your employees for failing to sell more combo meals, and to stop them from selling ninety-nine–cent items, you might take that off the menu. Obviously, this eventually would turn out to be a bad management decision—a decision that never would be made by a manager who spent time in the trenches.

The word from the watercooler is that we'd like to see you do this. By actually rolling up your sleeves and doing the job, you will not only get to know the task at hand better—you may also come up with effective suggestions for your subordinates. Again, you don't have to be the best at the job, but by being there in the trenches, you may see opportunities you would otherwise miss.

I recall watching my father-in-law build his house. He is an architect, so he designed the house himself. I'm sure he thought for years about how he wanted this house to end up, and as he designed the house he planned for every nook and cranny. However, once the house started to go up, he was able to see things that he liked and things he disliked. Because he was doing a lot of the building himself, he was able to say, "You know, I think I'm going to put an archway going into this room," or "Let's not put the recessed lighting in this corner." It was not in the original, well-thought-out plan, but because he was working in the trenches, he was able to see changes—both positive and negative—to the original design, all of which made the end product better.

As you spend time in the trenches, you too can see positive and negative changes that can help your peons be more effective in their work, and make your end product better. You will also find that spending more time in the trenches makes your people more comfortable with you, and they will bring you legitimate concerns and feedback. They will come to see you as an expert and as a coach. On the other hand, you might gain some respect for the job they do, and you may think twice the next time you are tempted to increase their workload.

As a worker who spends every workday in the trenches, I see firsthand how important it is for a boss who wants respect from his peons to spend some time with mud on his face. A leader who spends all day in an office, up on an elevated perch, gets no respect from anyone but their own ego.

I understand that, for some managers, my suggestion to spend time in the trenches goes into the "Nice to do, but impossible" pile. Often the position limits you, and you are unable to spend time in the trenches. If you can spend time in the trenches, do; if you can't, don't. But if you can't and don't, then don't give your peons feedback on how they do their specific jobs. You can deal with the people over which you have direct authority, but don't give me feedback directly related to my job performance if I have never seen you in the trenches.

Avoid the mistake made by my high school principal;

blanket authority over someone doesn't automatically give you the right to give direct feedback. Feedback, when required, should be given only by the peon's direct manager. In other words, if you are a vice president with whom I don't have any normal direct contact, and you walk by my desk and see me playing solitaire, don't say anything. I know that goes against your judgment. I know you are thinking to yourself, "That lazy slob! I paid to train him, I pay his benefits, I pay his salary, and this is what I get? If I have my way, his children's children's children won't be allowed to work at this company!"

While you may be right in thinking that, I will not respect your feedback—nor will I respect you as a person—if you lay into me, because I don't know you and I don't trust your ability to judge my work. Instead, complain to my direct manager and let her deal with me. Let my manager find out what I was doing, and my explanation. Follow up with her in a week and make sure she told me everything you would have—just don't tell me yourself. You will be much more effective, and you will be more trustworthy in both my eyes and my manager's. Just as it is taboo for a peon to go over his manager's head and skip rungs on the management ladder on certain issues, it is also bad business for a manager to skip a rung on the way down.

**Peons shouldn't go over a manager's head, and managers shouldn't go under another manager's head.**

Once again, it all boils down to respect. Spending time in the trenches will give you respect for the job your peons perform. It will also enable you to be more personal with the peons and to get to know and respect them on a personal level. In turn, when peons see you in the trenches they will respect you and the job you are trying to perform. As time goes on, the respect will evolve into trust and you will be able to develop a true, mutually beneficial co-worker relationship.

A great example of this was shown to me by one of the best managers I ever worked for. We will call him "El Supremo." *Mr.* Supremo really enjoyed being in the trenches. He had once owned his own investment company; he was talented, successful, educated, and refined. He had every reason in the world to just sit back, let us do the work, and take all the credit for it. However, he considered himself a true co-worker, and he saw great benefit to himself as a manager in doing the job we were doing. He seemed to see that we all had things to contribute to the team, and though he didn't hang out with us on the weekend, he prized our individuality. You got the impression that he felt that he could learn something from each of us.

For all I know, that could have just been charisma and secretly he thought we were all a bunch of rats. But I don't think so, because he spent time with us. He worked on the floor with us, made calls to customers, and complained about stupid company policy, just like the rest of us. Mostly, though, he went to lunch with us.

I know this seems like a simple, stupid thing, but I have worked at places where managers eat with managers and peons eat with peons. Not good. Look at what that does: It creates status-based segregation. In contrast, every day at about

10:00 A.M. El Supremo piped up, "So where are we going to lunch today?" I know that some managers believe talking about lunch at 10:00 A.M. shows weakness and a serious lack of dedication. However, E.S. understood the value of spending time with his people—particularly away from the office, where we were free to speak honestly.

He didn't have to do this, of course. He could have gone to lunch with the bigwigs every day. It would have probably helped him out with future promotions. They invited him, but sometimes he refused because he already had plans with the peons.

Some managers feel that if they go to lunch with the peons that they have to buy lunch. However, even though El Supremo made more money than the rest of us, there was no pressure to buy lunch for everybody. We all understood the principle of paying for our own meals. So, although sometimes we would go to a nice sit-down Mexican restaurant, other days we went to Jack-in-the-Box. He understood we didn't have the money to spend fifteen dollars on lunch every day, and he was cool with it. He was just as happy eating a forty-nine-cent taco as a ten-dollar chimichanga. He enjoyed being with his people. He was one of them. He wasn't a boss; he was a co-worker, a team leader, and the rest of us truly respected him for it.

As a result, if he had come to us and said, "Things are going to change a little bit—as of today, we are going to start selling fake vomit to hospitals," we'd have done it. Sure, we would complain, but because we trusted and respected Señor

Supremo, we would follow his lead. We were willing to follow him because he was a true leader. We never had to say, "I'd like to see you do this," because he was already doing it.

There is no reason to manage from afar. There is no logical reason not to base your management style in the trenches. Keep in mind that, for the most part, management is a non-revenue–generating position; in general, managers don't make any money for the company. Certainly, they can save a company's money, but they generate no direct revenue just by performing the managerial function. This is especially true of middle management. If a manager needs to maximize profits, and can't generate any additional revenue, then the manager must cut costs. This is about the only way most managers affect the company's bottom line.

Recall, however, that it's the peons of the world that generate revenue. Peons sell or market to get new revenue, they provide the finished product for sale, and they service the customer to protect that gained revenue. As a result, peons are less expendable to a company than management—and don't think that we peons don't realize it. This is why labor unions can be so powerful. The minute the peons stop working, and all that remains is management, work stops. If you need more proof, think about the last time your company had a massive layoff or asked for early retirements. Chances are, the most-affected segment of the company was middle management. In essence, the company had decided that it could run more efficiently without those managers than with them.

Thus, in addition to the benefit to your peons, being an in-the-trenches manager makes good sense for your own job security. Don't get caught with your finger up your nose. Don't get caught being expendable. Be a manager who is so integrated in the day-to-day operations of the peons that you are not easily removed.

I remember my high school football coach, during one of his more subdued halftime speeches, remarking, "Hey, I can't win this game for you. Although I'd love to, I can't make one tackle. I can't catch one touchdown pass. I am stuck on the sidelines. If we are going to win this game, you are going to have to do it."

As a manager, you don't want to get stuck in that situation. Obviously, there were rules preventing my coach from putting on shoulder pads and joining us; however, there are no rules preventing you from strapping on a headset or a hairnet and joining the peons.

**Lead, don't manage; help, don't coach; show, don't tell.**

### Creative Performing

Another reason it is important for managers to get in the trenches is that it helps them realize how unreasonable and ridiculous some of the goals they set can be, and how unrealistic expectations force their peons into *creative performing*. I know nobody will admit it, but in every job, everywhere, people get creative in order to meet unreasonable demands. People find a way to bend rules or to work around rules in order to meet the high performance standards set by management. Basically, the law of creative performing is that for every management action, there is an equal and opposite employee reaction.

**Management says, "Jump!" and employees say, "Okay, there has got to be a way to make the water splash, and make it look like we jumped, without actually jumping."**

In some cases, the goal set by management is simply impossible to attain. When that happens, employees are forced to resort to creative performance, to make a difficult decision between bending the rules and losing their job. For most people (even the honest ones), bending the rules is the more acceptable path of the two. Therefore, they get creative.

The pattern exists in almost all companies. Managers have to look good, and they don't look good if they don't set increasingly higher goals. As a result, they increase these goals every year, regardless of the peons' ability to accomplish the goals. The peons must then figure out a way to increase their production.

In most cases, do the people just work twice as hard? Do they stretch themselves a little more? Do they really respond to the manager's request to double production for the good of the company? No. People's capacity to perform the function has not increased. Simply raising the bar doesn't make them say, "Yippee! Now I can work harder." Instead, the response is generally, "Great. How am I supposed to reach those goals? I'm already putting in an extra hour every day just to get my work done. But if I don't make these new goals, I'll be fired. I better figure out a way to make it look like I am reaching those goals."

A manager increases goals, the people respond by fudging a little to reach those goals, the manager looks good because his manager sees the numbers, and everyone is happy. Except the peon. She is the one forced to fudge here and there, to make management think she is compliant with outrageous goals. She is the one unwillingly compromising her integrity in order to keep her job. She is the one feeling bad about herself, unable to come up with an acceptable compromise. Ironically, management's response to the situation is usually to raise goals a little higher. Heck, we doubled production last week, we ought to be able to double it again this week, right?

On the other hand, what is the managerial response when the peons don't meet the new lofty goals set for them? That it is the peons' fault! They just didn't work hard enough. Don't automatically jump to that conclusion.

**Instead, why not consider that the goals you set may indeed be unrealistic?**

It may seem that I am suggesting management forces people to lie. In a sense, that is what I am saying. In fact, I personally struggle with this issue. I consider myself to be an honest person, and I try to be straightforward with people. But I must also provide for my family, and my family is first on my list, even above myself. When I am presented with work situations where I must choose between bending the rules or being fired, I bend the rules. Is that dishonest? Yes. Is that wrong? Maybe.

But my responsibility to put bread on the table creates great pressure for me to have a job, and you can bet I'll work my hardest to reach the goals given me. If I have honestly worked my hardest, and I still can't reach the goals presented, then I must fudge.

Can you, with one hundred percent honesty, tell me that you are honest in all your business dealings? I doubt it. I know everyone has been put in some similar sort of situation, where the only way to meet an unreasonable goal is to "do the corporate thing" and fudge a little.

A friend of mine found himself in such a position during the summer between my junior and senior years of high school—a particularly nonproductive time for me. By the time I got around to looking for a summer job, about the only ones left were telemarketing positions. I took one with an obnoxious company that sold magazine subscriptions over the phone. This first introduction to the corporate working world was not a fun one. Back before people had caller ID and voice mail screeners, they used to just pick up the phone—and hang up on telemarketers. Occasionally, they would unload a profanity first. About one week into this job, I got lucky: I sold a subscription. I was on the board, and all of a sudden I had earned favor with the boss.

When a friend of mine, we'll call him "El Loco," came to me with a similar summer problem to my own, I got him a job working at the same company. We enjoyed carpooling to work and eating lunch together, but it soon became apparent that this job wasn't going to work out for him. After a couple of weeks, he started to get the feeling his neck was on the cutting block. He had been working almost three weeks with no sales. In that type of environment, no sales means no job.

The manager pulled El Loco into his office and said he must be doing something wrong; there was no reason he shouldn't have sold fifty magazine subscriptions by that time. The manager set a goal for El Loco: Sell five magazine subscriptions by the end of the week or El Loco would become El Jobless. Talk about some great goal setting! None in three weeks, but five in three days?

Obviously, El Loco felt the pressure. He had to get the sales. He had been doing everything he knew possible—he was working hard and trying hard—but not getting the sale. Now, though, something had to change.

I was, therefore, not as surprised as I should have been when I overheard the following exchange between Loco and a customer: "Hi, my name is El Loco with B and S Magazine Company. I would like to interest you in... Yes... Yes, I understand... Okay, sure. Well, listen: I know this deal isn't that great and you don't want it, but I am going to lose my job if you don't buy something. Will you please just act like you are buying it—go through the buying process, and then just cancel your subscription right after you get off the phone? That way I can keep my job and you don't have to buy any magazines."

Well, the customer didn't buy anything and the unfortunate Mr. Loco did eventually become El Jobless. But this is a good example of what I am talking about. El Loco is a very honest, trustworthy, hardworking guy. Nevertheless, if you put people up against a wall, sometimes through no fault of their own, they will do anything to protect their job. Often, the fear of unemployment is much more fierce than the fear of sinning or being caught in a lie. Too often, otherwise honest, hardworking people will find some way to show that they did what you asked.

Another easy visualization of creative performance might be found in construction. The foreman wants a house done by a certain time to meet financial deadlines, so he tells the workers to get it done "yesterday." Under this kind of pressure, the workers may not take time to ensure that the job is done correctly; the goal set does not allow for that. Instead, they do what they are told, and the house gets finished quickly—poorly, but on time.

**Peons will do what they must.**

If the goal is to keep their job, people will do what they must to keep in good standing with the boss. A good manager must strive to make sure that goals are reasonable and reachable, to keep their employees from straying toward creative performance. You don't have to make the goals easy, just make them realistic. The only true way to know if they are realistic is by spending time in the trenches, striving for those goals personally, and coming up short. Don't use a spreadsheet or a pie graph to tell you where your goals should be; spend time in the trenches in order to ensure that you are getting real performance, not the creative kind.

After college, I drew on my experience as a telephone sales agent and accepted a job at an inside sales office. This was a more glorified, salaried version of a telemarketer. It actually was a nice job, and that division of the company was doing very well; in fact, it was the most successful sales group in the company. However, like many other companies, that company presented the peons with the opportunity to bend or be fired.

In that office, for instance, one of the judging criteria was for each salesperson to have twenty-one sales calls per day. Couple those twenty-one calls with preparing and sending out proposals, relationship maintenance, and some customer service, and twenty-one calls constitutes a full day's work. When management found that our group was successful with this model, they were thrilled.

But then they started to think about it. My guess is that the thought went something like this: "We are at 110 percent now, and we only average twenty-one calls. Let's get them to make more calls and that will increase our numbers. Let's set the goal at twenty-five calls, and I'm sure that will turn into 200 percent for us."

That makes sense, right? If productivity is good, double the goals, and productivity will double too! Hooray!

As I said, though, simply increasing the goal doesn't necessarily increase a peon's capacity to reach that goal. It's as if I just finished running a seven-minute mile, only to have some-one come up to me and tell me, "Okay, you used to run it in nine, and now you run seven, so the next time you run it, you should be able to do it in five minutes." Sorry, it doesn't work that way, and if managers spent more time in the trenches, they would know better.

At this company, then, the employees faced an ethical dilemma: How do we perform the function required and still make these goals? People said to themselves, "If I had to work very hard to get everything done and still was only able to make twenty-one calls, how am I going to maintain the quality of my sales while increasing the quantity?"

At first, we peons attempted to do both, to meet the goals and still perform the job function to the best of our abilities. We tried to believe that we could do it. We were motivated by managerial speeches about success and glory, but it soon became apparent that meeting the goal was just not possible. It was impossible to keep up the same level of service to the cus-tomer and to increase productivity at the same time. I guess if a peon worked twelve-hour days he might be able to get it all done. Unfortunately, we weren't paid enough to put in twelve-hour days, so we were left to find some sort of compromise in the situation.

The compromise ended up being our integrity. People found ways to make it look like they were making twenty-five calls when in fact they were really only making the same twen-ty-one quality calls per day. People found new ways around the system, ways to make the goals and keep their managers happy.

Of course, the managers never questioned our method of obtaining the numbers. They just went to their senior manager and showed they were successful in getting their people to make 25 calls. They had challenged their peons to respond at a higher level, and their peons delivered. In reality, though, all the managers accomplished was to make their people dishonest and to lower theemployee job satisfaction level. The employees were performing the same job as before, only now we had to spend a little extra time figuring out where and how to fudge our numbers. The numbers went up, productivity stayed the same, and morale went down.

I've seen the most honest people get a little creative with the rules, buckling under the pressure to make the goal. I'll bet if you look real hard inside yourself and evaluate your work very thoroughly, you'll find some areas where you bent the rules a little—got a little creative—in order to make your boss happy. You'll recall jobs where you missed a few spots just to get the work done fast, rather than getting it done right. It is something that seems to exist at every workplace, unfortunately. Sometimes the goals are so high that even if we had our best day every day, we wouldn't reach them. So we do what we have to for job preservation.

The thing is, creative performance is unnecessary if peons are presented with reachable goals. However, in most situations, management sets the goals for employees without input from the two most important sources: the employees themselves, and a good working knowledge of the job itself. Accurate, reachable goals cannot be set with a prediction model; they can only be set by people actually doing the work. When you set goals for your peons, then, at least consult with the people who are going to have to accomplish that goal. They know their capability, and you might be surprised at their willingness to increase goals. But let them help to decide.

This is yet another important reason to spend time in the trenches. Spending time in their shoes will help you get a clearer vision of what your peons can do. When you spend time in their shoes, you will see that raising production from eighty to one hundred percent isn't just a piece of cake. You'll be able to set reasonable, workable goals, so that your people aren't forced into the realm of creative performance. Creative performance is averted when managers evaluate real working conditions, plan for realistic growth, and formulate realistic goals.

**People will work for a goal they feel is attainable. They will cheat to reach a goal they feel is unattainable.**

Another great way to keep people honest is to acknowledge the fact that they are sometimes forced to be dishonest—though this should not be done in a negative or disciplinary way. If you know that everybody on your team is fudging their numbers a little (and they are), acknowledge their method for doing so. Then ask them what you can do to avoid forcing them to do that. Some possible approaches include:

"I don't want to make you be dishonest."

"Why is this being done?"

"What can I do to change things to help you report more honest numbers?"

However you approach the issue, assure the peon that her job is not in jeopardy and that you aren't going to write her up for talking to you about this. Now, maybe you won't get an acceptable response, or maybe the power to change the unrealistic requirements is in hands above yours. Nonetheless, acknowledging the situation will help your people be more open, it will show the peons that you empathize, and it will inspire somebody, either you or them, to come up with a solution to the problem.

Maybe you don't care if your people aren't completely honest. Maybe you fudge things yourself, or you slack a little here and there (and you probably do). Maybe your philosophy is, "I don't care what they do, as long as they get me over one hundred percent and into the eagle's nest." And maybe you get away with that kind of attitude, for now. In the long run, though, that kind of attitude will destroy a company. That attitude filters down to your employees, who may take the same approach with your company's customers, which will upset the customers and cause them to leave. You will have employees dissatisfied with their jobs, you will have customers upset with their service, and in time, your business will suffer.

At one point in my career, I worked as a pool man. In this capacity, I cleaned the pools of a number of customers each week. The pay for the job was distributed on a per-pool basis—

I got five dollars for every pool I cleaned. When I trained for the position, the person training me informed me that I wanted to get each pool done quickly so that I could make more money per hour. While I started out with this intention, I soon noticed that some pools took one or more hours to complete, if I wanted to do a good job. It didn't seem right that I would get less per hour if I did a great job cleaning the pools.

I was able to discuss this with the manager, and her response was the right one: "I want you to do a good job. I realize that the way it is set up, you are not rewarded for doing a good job. If you find that some pools are taking longer than forty-five minutes, let me know and we'll compensate you for that." She then changed the policy for all the pool cleaners, acknowledging that she would rather have them do a good job than to meet the goals unethically. After that, you saw some pretty happy guys driving around with a pole sticking out of the back of their truck.

In that situation, the manager realized that the goal-setting process was flawed, but she also made the decision to reward the most important goal, which was doing the right thing for the customer. By making this choice, she also helped me to be more satisfied in my work and enabled me to take more pride in the work I was asked to perform.

Please, managers, spend time in the trenches. By spending time in the trenches, you will earn the respect of your people, as well as develop a good knowledge of the job they do every day. That way you can more effectively coach and instruct them and set more effective goals. When you accomplish that, your people won't need to engage in creative performing, and you will have a more open, honest workplace with a higher level of employee morale. Sure, your face may get a little dirty, and sure, you may ruin that nice pair of shoes. But you will be much more effective when you get in the trenches, and your people will work harder for you in return.

((

# Get Feedback

Feedback. You wear this managerial tool like a gun on your hip. Any time, any place you see something wrong at the workplace, you are ready and willing to let the peons know exactly . . . . .

## Chapter Five

. . . . . **where they slipped up**. You love to give feedback. Many times, it just rolls off your tongue without even having to think about it. Even in situations where other managers have no feedback to give, you somehow are able to identify errant behavior.

When you are on a roll, the words magically seem to penetrate the mind of your subordinates, and you can almost physically see the change in their behavior. Sometimes you find yourself at your desk at the end of the day, thinking back on the day's work, and that one bit of feedback you gave stands out in your mind like a white robe at a heavy metal rock concert. What you told Jason in response to his unacceptable work was just perfect, almost poetic. You think to yourself that you ought to write it down and send it in to the training department so that when they write the new management training modules, they'll put you in there. With your ability to provide feedback, it's a wonder they didn't promote you to management sooner. Feedback is so easy—I'm sure you'd say it's the easiest, most rewarding, most fun part of your job.

Oh, wait. This chapter is titled "*Get* Feedback," not "Give Feedback." But that must be a typo. You are thinking to yourself, "I am a manager. I don't get feedback; I give it. I don't think I've received feedback from a peon since, well… Wait a second—I don't think I've ever received feedback from a peon! Ha ha ha!"

Peon-generated feedback seems like a rather absurd subject, doesn't it?

I mean, what could a peon tell you about being a manager? It's not as if they could come up with a book of suggestions or anything.

Actually, getting good, constructive feedback from your peons may be just what you need to be a more successful manager. Quality feedback can be a gauge that allows you to see where you are as a manager, as opposed to where you think you are. For some reason, however, it seems to be human nature to avoid asking for quality feedback. For example, morons like me would rather drive fourteen miles in a circle than ask for directions. Others of us hate going to the dentist because we'll be told we need to floss more often.

Many times, too, when we ask for feedback we ask loaded questions that prevent the other party from giving us an honest answer. Like when your spouse asks, "Does my butt look big in these spandex pants?"

"Of course not, honey. You look great."

"You're lying."

"Why would I lie about that?"

"You know my butt is huge."

"Okay, you have a big butt."

"You are such a jerk. What do you expect me to look like after giving birth to your children?"

Such ineffective dialogues aren't limited to personal relationships. Asking for workplace feedback can be just as ineffective, for instance, if you ask for feedback but then force your preferred answer. I have heard managers ask things like, "It says here I'm supposed to ask you what I can do to help you. So, there's not anything, right? Okay, great." It is not feedback if you give us the answer. Ask the question and then shut your mouth. Let us tell you how we truly feel; don't assume you already know.

I know the very thought makes the hair on the back of your neck stand up, but feedback is critical if you want to succeed at anything, especially at management. The wonderful thing is, if you get accurate feedback, it will be much more effective than reading any book. Good, bottom-to-top feedback is more effective than any weeklong management seminar in Vegas. It will create better results, faster, than making sweeping personnel changes. It will help efficiency much more quickly and more thoroughly than some Six Sigma strategy. You won't have to read books about cheese, about influencing people, or about peons, because you will know exactly what is going on in your company, and you will be able to identify solutions to problems. Each company, each employee, and each situation is different.

**The only way to get a truly 20/20 view of how to be the best manager in your company, with your group of peons, with the current situation, is to ask the peons themselves.**

In order to get good feedback, though, you need to give people an environment conducive to feedback, and you need to ask—no, *beg*—for honest, effective feedback. Surrounding yourself with yes-people does nothing but enlarge your ego. It will not lead to progress, nor is it healthy for the company. Ask for true, honest feedback from your people, and if they aren't honest, ask yourself why. Find a way to get that honest feedback. If you must, then distribute anonymous questionnaires, have other managers interview your people, put on a wig and a mustache and act like a window cleaner. No matter how you accomplish it, come up with some way to get honest, effective feedback from your people.

And once again, don't bring up your "open door policy" with me. Be honest: How many people would have the guts to walk into your office, to say, "Hey, can I have a second?", and then to sit down and tell you what a terrible job you are doing, without fear of retribution? The only peons stupid enough to do that are either already on their way out or are taking a management class at the local community college.

**I don't care how open your front door is. The implied fear of most peons is that the back door is also open.**

Some peons will even say, "I don't care if she is a terrible manager. As long as I get my paycheck every two weeks, I won't say anything."

Most of us are so afraid of losing our jobs, or of losing the ability to get that next promotion because a review says, "Dave has a negative attitude," that we don't give any feedback. We'd rather be the good corporate citizen you want us to be and maintain the status quo.

Many managers don't really seek out good, honest feedback because they don't really want to receive it. If you are the type who doesn't really want it, then why not? What are you afraid of? You may have to eat a slice of humble pie, but that will be worth it if it will help you take your management to the next level. You are going to have to be able to take the feedback and use it wisely, even if it is directed negatively toward you. Remember, you'll never get better without it.

I'm sure you are saying to yourself, "I know I need feedback, and I welcome it." But do you really? Watch yourself the next time someone gives you constructive criticism. Do you find yourself defending every minor accusation? Do you get flustered and upset? Most importantly, what do you do with the recommendations? Do you convince yourself that it is just one person's isolated opinion? Do you stigmatize the person and label them *negative*? Worst of all, do you just play it down and basically throw the suggestion in the garbage? If you find yourself handling feedback this way, then you've got it all wrong. Here's some feedback for you: You need to change your attitude about feedback. Think of yourself as a sponge for feedback, rather than as a punching bag.

Even more importantly, once you get the honest feedback, your peons must see that you are doing something with it. If I give you honest feedback and tell you that your motivational quotes for every situation bother me, and then your next e-mail contains some quote about flocks of eagles, I will know you didn't take my feedback seriously. If I come to that conclusion, I am forever cured of the desire to give you honest feedback.

Like most employees, I generally start out new jobs full of hope that this will finally be my dream job. Without fail, I begin by coming up with ideas, suggestions, and insights that I feel might help the company. At some point, though, each manager has shown disinterest in my ideas, or passed them off as rookie talk. My response, then, is to shut the vault of ideas. Occasionally, just when I think I'm respected and my opinion matters, I might try to open the vault again. Unfortunately, it generally is closed once again, due to some indifference on some scale.

Now, maybe my ideas were terrible and didn't have merit. But in the interest of the employee and the company, a manager should address any idea without prejudice, and then explain why that idea won't work, if that's the case. Recognize that if an employee is coming up with ideas, they are trying to help the company. Reward them for that, if only through positive recognition. You don't have to take their suggestion, but it would be a good idea to explain why. And "because I said so, and I am the boss" is not an explanation.

**Keep in mind that the spirit in which you receive our feedback is the same spirit in which we peons will receive yours.**

### Run with It

I did work at one company where my boss showed interest in my feedback and ideas, and it was a great example of how showing that kind of interest can be good for the company and good for the morale and excitement of the employee. When I first joined that company, I was very unimpressed with their sales presentation literature. Basically, it comprised photocopies of some bulleted sheets produced on a typewriter. It looked terrible. So I went home and played around with the print program on my computer, and I came back with more visually pleasing materials. They were not high-class documents, by any means, but they were a start. Slowly, I developed a vision that included a Web site, a professional trade show display, and much more professionally created mailers and brochures.

After accomplishing all this, I went to the boss and I gave him my ideas. He had two options at that point. First, since he was the one that had come up with the original typewritten stuff, he could have taken offense and pooh-poohed my suggestions. The second option was to recognize that I had worked on this stuff at home, to note that I was willing to do additional work to get the project done, and to let me run with it.

Well, he let me run with it. Not only did he appreciate the feedback I had given him, he also got behind my suggestions. He got a new computer installed in my office, with whatever software I requested, he gave me a nicer title, and he started to consult me on his advertising ventures. I know it seems ridiculous, but he made me feel special. Because of this, I felt obligated to come up with more ideas, to see that the ideas were put in place, and to help the company succeed.

I did this extra work and spent this extra time, all without a salary increase. I still didn't get benefits, I still didn't get vacation time, and there was still no gym at the office. Nonetheless, because I saw my ideas implemented, I took ownership of the work. My motivation came from the fact that this company respected its peons and took feedback seriously. My dedication was based primarily on the owner's ability to take feedback, to respect it, to filter it, and to run with the good points. Sometimes he'd tell me my ideas were crap, and that was okay. But I have not seen a manager since who was so willing to listen to new ideas, or who had the confidence in himself to ask for honest feedback from his workers. My satisfaction from my work was so great that I stayed at a low-paying job with no vacation time or benefits for over two years, much longer than I should have.

I'm sure you've seen new employees come to work all fired up with new ideas and suggestions, only to seemingly become just like everyone else after a while. This typically happens because nobody takes the employee's feedback and suggestions seriously, and after a while the employee stops giving it. When you receive feedback, do something with it, acknowledge the suggestions, tell us you are working on them. Let us see a change wrought in our office that was initiated by a piece of our feedback. Let us see that you really appreciate and take seriously the feedback given. If we are able to see that you as managers really want feedback, and will use it, and that this isn't just some corporate mandate designed to get the company some Peon 9001 certification, then we will give you more.

### Check Engine

Getting feedback isn't as easy as putting a sign on your door saying "Suggestions welcome." To receive effective feedback, you need to ask specific questions. Please, don't do the ol' "So, how do you feel things are going?" Have you ever heard anything other than "Fine" or "Great"? Of course you haven't.

Even worse, don't ask, "Do you have any feedback for me?" As one speaking from the peon side of the desk, who always had many suggestions, it is much easier to just say no than to say, "Well, actually…."

Instead, ask specific questions like, "What is your opinion about the way we are handling the X project?" or "I'm not sure our meetings have been as effective as I would like. What do you think I could do better?" or "I know you keep hearing that the numbers are down, and I know why my boss is saying they are down, but what is your opinion?"

Think of feedback as the engine indicator light on your car. Sometimes we see that there is a problem, but the only information we get is "Check Engine." Well, what does that mean? It could be anything. How much more effective would it be if your peons' feedback were more like "Battery" or "Door Ajar." Getting specific, honest feedback will allow you to address problems quickly, efficiently, and effectively. When the only feedback you see is high turnover or generally low employee morale, it is like the Check Engine light: You know there is a problem, but you have no idea how to fix it. You might have some theories, but there is really only one way to know for sure—get under the hood and get good, straightforward, specific feedback.

Take the approach that the peons may be the experts on the subject at hand, then ask them for an expert opinion. They will appreciate that you are opening up the channel for feedback, and they will trust you more, knowing that you think they are worthy enough to be an expert and to give advice. Try it; you may be surprised by the floodgates of feedback opening wide. All that pent-up advice finally will be given an avenue for effective use.

When you receive feedback, ask yourself, Is this something I can fix? If so, how easily and how do I do it? If the issue is something you cannot fix, discuss the feedback with the giver and tell them why you won't be using it. In your own mind, prioritize the feedback received, and filter it to find the truly effective feedback.

"Check Engine" is pretty vague, but by seeking out effective feedback, you can nearly always find the real problem. I once had an issue where the feedback from my car wasn't specific enough. I stuck the keys in the ignition, but no matter how many times I turned the key, and no matter how much or how little I pumped the gas pedal, the dang thing wouldn't start. One person said it must be the alternator. Fearing an expensive repair and a wasted weekend spent under the hood, I hoped that person was wrong. Another person suggested that I needed a new battery. Maybe, but that can also be an expensive and time-consuming operation. Finally, a wise person asked me, "Are you sure your battery terminals are connected?" Sure enough, one of the electrical connectors to the battery had loosened. Simply tightening a nut solved the problem. Had I gone with either of the other two suggestions, I would have spent a lot of time and money repairing a working alternator or replacing a fully functioning battery.

How many times do you do something similar as a manager? How many times do you follow your intuition, or the advice of some consultant, rather than looking for advice from your employees? Sometimes the fix is something quick and inexpensive. Sometimes you don't need to redo everything. The only way you'll know that, though, is by starting out easy and asking your employees.

My experience with my car demonstrates that solving a problem doesn't necessarily need to be difficult. That's why, when you call computer tech support, the first thing they ask is, "Did you turn the machine on?" It seems mundane, but sometimes, oddly enough, that is the answer to the problem. Rather than go to great lengths to fix the wrong thing, get feedback from your employees to find out where the real problems are.

Start today: elicit specific feedback. If you don't have that kind of relationship with your employees, then in order to get good feedback—at least initially—you are going to have to make it anonymous. Maybe those peons have nothing to fear. Maybe they won't get fired if they tell you that they can't stand your management style, but they may not know that. Until they are convinced that feedback is truly welcome, they won't give you completely honest answers.

If you must, then, start by setting up a truly anonymous

system for feedback—and not the little suggestion box by the coffee pot either. Quit wimping out on me. What I mean is, once each month give your peons ten free minutes out of their workday to complete an anonymous survey. Don't take any of our personal time, take up work time, and if it's possible, have us use a computer, so we won't be worried you'll figure out our handwriting. Don't set up an internal Web site—we'll be afraid you can track which computer is making those entries. The best method is a word processing document, printed out and turned in to an anonymous box. I know, this is more work for you, but remember, this will get you truly honest feedback.

And again, once you get feedback, address it. Let us see that you appreciate it. You too can get your employees to take ownership of their projects. You too can get more out of your employees without increasing pay or benefits. You too can run a more efficient ship by seeking out and using good, honest feedback. Sure, you can still give it occasionally, too. I'll give you that. But you should be asking for as much as you are giving, if not more.

**There is no better source about how to be a good manager for your team than the team members themselves.**

Take advantage of this valuable resource, and make it work for you.

☾

# Get Organized

In my neck of the woods, tradition dictates that on Thanksgiving morning we play football. Some play tackle football, others two-hand touch, and others are organized . . . . .

## Chapter Six

. . . . . **enough to have flags**. Family against family, brother against brother, everyone plays football on Thanksgiving. We call it the Turkey Bowl. Wannabes from every walk of life get together on an elementary or junior high school field to claim glory and bragging rights for an entire year.

A few years back, however, a few of my friends and I decided to skip the annual Turkey Bowl game in favor of the Turkey Trot. While the titles share the same first name, the two events couldn't be more different. The Turkey Trot is an annual 10K run put on by the local city Parks and Recreation Department, and it's a pretty serious run. We, of course, were not very serious about it; we just heard that in order to get a T-shirt you had to outrun some guy dressed in a turkey outfit. No problem.

We arrived about ten minutes before the start of the 7:00 A.M. race and immediately realized we were in way over our heads. Competing runners turned out from the various colleges in the area, for instance, and for some reason we were the only ones wearing jeans and button-down shirts for the race. My friend was wearing a pair of flip-flops, and I was unsure how my loafers were going to handle ten kilometers of running. You know, in the United States they really don't teach us the metric system, and we were kind of under the impression that a 10K wasn't much longer than one hundred yards.

Trying to capitalize on a difficult situation, I told my buddy, Spencer that I was going to win the race. He replied that his only desire was to just lead the race, even for just a second. I thought that idea was a much better, more reachable goal, so we accepted that as our strategy for the race.

Because of our late arrival and registration, we were placed at the very back of the enormous pack of people. Soon the gun sounded—the beginning of the race. There were so many people in the race, however, that we stood there for a while and nobody around us moved. Soon we realized that this was because we were waiting, like cars in rush hour, for the wave of movement to reach us. By the time we were even able to run, people in the front of the race had already been running for a minute or so.

Undaunted by the one-minute handicap, Spencer and I began to run as fast as we could, passing up many people—including the turkey guy—trying to get to the front of the pack, if only for a moment. Just at the point that our legs started to feel like Jell-O and our minds started to abandon this silly goal, we saw the front of the pack. I yelled to Spencer that there he was: The Guy In Front. All we had to do was pass him.

We dropped gears and accelerated to a full sprint. The denim of my jeans started to heat up from friction, and Spencer had lost both his flip-flops. We pushed forward, Spencer reaching first as I ran behind him. I saw him turn his head and thrust his fist into the air in success. He was first in the race. He couldn't say anything because he was out of breath, and his bare feet struggled to keep the pace of these professional runners, but he nodded as if to say, "I have done it! I have conquered Kilimanjaro!" Then he dropped back to give me a chance to bask in the light of the lead.

I used all my energy to accelerate to a point where now I was first in the race. Of the thousands of people running that day, I was, if only for a second, the fastest one. I felt empowered for a brief second, until my jeans started to smoke and my left loafer lost its sole. Soon a wave of well-toned, scantily clad people in their Oakley sunglasses passed me as if I was standing still.

Slowly, one by one, they passed, and we moved farther back in the pack. Spencer and I had enjoyed our time in the lead, and now we were dropping places fast. The flaw in our strategy became clear when we discovered we were now too tired to run at even a normal pace. We had expended so much energy on a meaningless goal—now we were going to be lucky to even complete the race. Soon, average runners were passing us. Before long, we were falling behind little kids and a guy on crutches.

## Create the Vision

Why do I tell you this story? Beyond the self-deprecation, there are actually some lessons here. First, make sure that all of your goals are rooted in getting you to your ultimate goal. Our goal to occupy first place for at least a second really accomplished nothing. We would have done better if our objectives revolved around some sort of goal at the end of the race.

Think about the way you manage your team—are you more concentrated on the process or on the result? Are your peons' goals and the verification process used taking them toward a meaningless accomplishment, or are the goals actually helping them reach some true goal? Get your people to the end of the race, rather than just occupying first place for a meaningless piece of it. If you spend time verifying that your people are doing the process, they will do the process. On the other hand, when you make sure they understand the end goal, they will be more likely to get there.

If you manage a customer service team, for example, are your goals all centered around getting off the phone within a certain time? How about setting up a reward system for people who make customers so happy that the customer calls back to tell you how great their representative was? If you are working in a fast-food restaurant, are you so worried about setting the time record for order processing that you serve hamburgers with croutons and salads topped with ketchup?

I understand that short-term goals are intended to get you to your end goal, but are your short-term goals accomplishing that? Perhaps if Spencer and I had set short-term Turkey Trot goals to be at a certain time interval at every mile or half mile, then we could have measurably hit a goal time for the entire race. We could have finished the race in a respectable fashion and accomplished an end goal. However, our meaningless goal got us nowhere near running a respectable race. All we did was waste a lot of energy, experience severe cramping, and ruin a perfectly good pair of loafers.

I know you think your processes are getting you there, but I can almost guarantee that your employees wouldn't agree. In their secret meetings, they say to each other, "Why does she spend so much time making sure that we do A or B? If she were smart, she would make us do X and Y, so we could get Z. The way she's going, the only thing we'll get is C."

The processes you ask your peons to work on are only as good as the results they get you, so why not spend time getting people to provide results, rather than focusing on processes?

**Ensure that no matter what you do or what processes you have in place, your people always understand how the daily process leads toward the desired result, and verify that the process is in fact taking them there.**

Don't just give people things to do every day; provide them with a vision and ensure that the daily processes fit into the vision.

The second point I wish to draw from the Turkey Trot story is the importance of using good organization to prepare. Had we taken time to organize our race plan, our clothing, and ourselves, Spencer and I could have avoided a lot of humiliation and soreness, as well as having more fun along the way. Being organized is crucial to the success of a good manager.

True organization will help you keep all the personal elements of your people sorted out. This, in turn, will present you as more trustworthy to your people, and when they trust you, they will follow you. Likewise, a true leader is organized in purpose and direction.

I hate all those lame sayings thrown around at work—you know, the ones that are supposed to be catchy and motivating:

"Let's synergize!" or "There is no *I* in *teamwork*." (Notice, however, that there is an *M* and an *E*.) I especially can't stand, "Let's think outside the box," "You need a vision," or, my personal favorite, "Excuse me, I believe you have my stapler."

Because I hate these types of sayings, I've particularly avoided adding any of that crap to my book. For this reason, when I am discussing managerial organization, I'm not going to tell you to "plan your work and work your plan." It is good advice, and it would fit in perfectly right here, but I'm not going to say it. I am also going to refuse to counsel you to "begin with the end in mind." Again, great wisdom, works well with our discussion, but a little too cliché for me. If I'm going to sell out that easily, I might as well say something like "Paralysis by analysis," "paradigm shift," or "going forward." Nope, not me. I will not compromise this book by including catchphrases like that.

Many such catchphrases focus on managerial organization, which makes sense. Good managerial organization will organize your vision for your team, create the path they must take, and give them the focus they need. This type of organization means creating a plan for the work that your team will do for the next month or year or two years or ten years, and then working that plan. It is about planning your work, and working your plan. It is about beginning with an end in mind, and ensuring that all the steps taken are leading to that end. Which, of course, is something I would never say.

It is important to point out that "organized" does not necessarily mean "clean," as anyone who has seen my desk can confirm. While I am not generally organized in the clean sense, I do like organization in the way I work. I am always walking around with a to-do list in my pocket. Obviously, it requires some organization to write this book while working two jobs, pursuing a master's degree, spending time with my wife and four kids, and attending to my house and church duties. So I am living proof that organized does not mean clean, and vice versa.

The first step in getting organized is to come up with a vision. This can sometimes be the hardest part—figuring out where you realistically want to be. Of course, you'd like your team to be first place among teams in every category, and to have every member of your team be happy, healthy, and rich. But be realistic. Determine a vision that is both attainable and measurable, and set objectives to be reached along the way that will lead you to your vision.

At the prodding of one of my managers, I once came up with an approach to creating a vision for our team. The vision was titled "Worst to First by May 31st." It's catchy, it's sexy, and it's easy to remember. The date chosen was May 31 because our fiscal year began June 1 and I figured that we should set the next fiscal year as our beacon on the horizon. That was our vision. It was reachable and it was measurable.

In order to implement my vision, I suggested that each month we create a theme designed to help us concentrate on things that would get us to first place. Then, each week, we'd have a more specific goal to concentrate on—that goal would get us to the monthly goal, which ultimately would get us to the yearly goal. I suggested that at the beginning of the week we should get together and review the goal from the previous week, discuss successes in accomplishing that goal, and then present the new week's goal and suggestions on how to attain it. Put in an outline form, this approach would look like this:

**Goal: Worst to First by May 31st**

**Month 1: Objectives that will help us get from worst to first**

    **Week 1: Objective that will help us accomplish Month 1 objectives**

    **Week 2: Objective**

    **Week 3: Objective**

    **Week 4: Objective**

**Month 2: Objective**

    **Week 1: Objective that will help us accomplish Month 2 objectives**

    **Week 2: Objective**

    **Week 3: Objective**

    **Week 4: Objective**

This pattern would then continue through the entire year. When the whole team bought into the plan, understood the vision, and believed in the end goal, it would be a real success. By organizing the vision and the work program, it would be much easier for the team to work together, to generate momentum, and then to ride the wave of weekly objectives to the shores of our vision.

The nice thing about presenting this type of organized vision is that while the themes change from week to week, so it's not one boring concentration, each theme constitutes the next step in reaching your vision. The only way to climb Mt. Everest is step by step, but you must make sure that each step is getting you up the mountain, not around it. My team had weekly and monthly processes to work on, but if they understood the overall vision, they would see how these processes were getting them to the end goal. They would then work on the processes with the end goal always lingering in the back of their minds.

As an example, let's say we manage a team of school bus drivers and want to reach the goal of "no accidents this school year," with each month divided into various elements of preventative safety. We make September Education month, and each week of September includes an individual task, all of which focus on educating people about safety procedures. The theme of Week 1 might be "educate the bus drivers," with all the bus drivers given a short-term goal of completing a training course in proper bus safety. In outline form, then, the plan might look like this:

**Goal: Zero Accidents This Year**

**September: Education**

**Week 1: Educate the bus drivers**

**Week 2: Educate the school staff**

**Week 3: Educate the children**

**Week 4: Educate the parents**

**October: Safety at bus stops**

    **Week 1: Pull the stop shield before you stop**

    **Week 2: Watch for running children**

    **Week 3: Check every mirror**

    **Week 4: Wait for all children to be seated before putting the bus in gear**

**November: Safety at intersections**

I think you can see how this might continue. Not only will this type of organization help to keep the work organized for the team, it will also keep the team itself organized. If the team members all understand the vision, they will all work together to reach that goal. They will help one another along the way, and they will work more closely as a team.

Thus, the first step in organizing your team is to create the vision, some sort of long-term goal. One year down the road, two years, whatever. It is preferable not to set a goal too far down the road, or your peons won't be interested; they will assume they'll never see the results. Again, involve your peons in the process of developing the goal. Use them not only to create the end goal, but also to build a system of objectives to be accomplished along the way.

Most importantly, keep in mind that each objective must somehow lead to the end goal, so evaluate each objective and determine if it serves that function. If I were to plan and organize a climb of Mt. Everest, for instance, I would not include "tie and untie my shoes sixteen times" in my list of daily objectives. I'm sure tying your shoes is a part of climbing Everest, but it is not a primary part of it. Instead, the goals should focus on climbing so many feet per day, or drinking so much water, or reaching certain points along the way—all goals that will get me there.

**If I spend all day tying and untying my shoes, I get no closer to the top of the mountain, and the only thing I accomplish is a pair of broken laces.**

Once you create the vision and determine what you want to accomplish in the end, then you must communicate it. Take time to make sure every peon understands the vision. Be organized in your communication. Find out if anyone has objections to or reservations about the vision. Communicate the weekly and monthly objectives associated with the vision. Verify that everybody on the team understands the vision, understands how the objectives will lead to the vision, and that they all buy in to the plan, agreeing that the objectives are helping you reach the vision.

Once you have the vision, and you've communicated it, then you must get a little more organized and come up with some sort of a map or calendar for everyone to follow. A map is appropriate if the end goal includes a series of progressions; it allows the peons to see how one step leads to the next, which eventually leads to the result. If your scenario is based on weekly and monthly goals, then put it all on a calendar or organize it in an outline form. This sort of visualization is key to constant communication of your vision.

Now that you have the vision, you've communicated it,

and you have a method for constant communication, stick to it. There is nothing worse than a manager working hard to come up with a great plan, creating diagrams and calendars to support that plan, and then, because of some cosmic rift in the galaxy somewhere, abandoning the idea and forgetting about it. Stay focused. If your vision was good and true, then there should be no reason for you to abandon it.

## Flavor of the Month

Create the goal, create the plan, communicate it, and stay focused on it. Avoid the "flavor of the month" trap of disorganization, which is the way most companies operate. When you subscribe to the flavor of the month, you are running the company by the seat of your pants. You have a vision one month, and then the next month the vision is something entirely different. Management says to employees, "This week I want everybody to worry about safety." Next week, though, you suddenly change your mind and decide you want everybody to concentrate on saving the company money. This lasts for two weeks, and then out of nowhere, your peons hear, "Production numbers are down; you all better bring them up or you're fired."

Well, maybe if we hadn't been spending so much time on safety and on saving money, we might have brought the numbers up. What are you, butter pecan, rainbow sherbet, or gooey chocolate? Make up your mind. Pick a style, pick a flavor, and stick to it.

**Pick a vision and stick to it.**

Pick a style of organization and stick to it. Don't come up with a new style or flavor every week.

Sometimes, of course, the company comes out with directives that you just have to follow, even though they are 180 degrees from the vision you originally created. In such a case, curse. Curse long and loud and with some flair, and when you're done, make some slight changes if you must, but don't abandon your vision just because the company has a new directive this week; instead, try to get that new directive to fit into your vision.

If it doesn't fit, then talk to your manager. Don't be afraid to stand up to your director or vice president. If she tells you she wants to see those shoes tied and untied twenty times a day, tell her to step back and look at the big picture. Tell her about your plan of focus and about how you want to stick to that because it is getting you to your end goal. If your vice president or director still can't see a way to fit their directives into your organized plan, then give them a copy of this book. If your ideas and vision are right in the first place, there should be no reason to abandon it.

Here's an example. Let's say you coach a football team, and during your preparations you determine that the way to beat the opponent in this week's game is to run the football on offense and play tough in the middle of the defense. At halftime you sit down to assess the first half. The game is tied 10-10, and your running game is moving along okay. You know you can outlast the other team, so you are confident that your game plan will work.

As you are sitting there, however, the team's owner comes up to you and says, "Why don't you throw a little more in the second half? I like to see you throw, and besides, we have that wide receiver we are paying $30 million a year. Get him the ball."

Now, you know the quarterback didn't look that great throwing the ball during practice that week, and you know that the other team's cornerback, who is covering your star wide receiver, is one of the best in the league. All the information you have tells you that a running game rather than a passing game will work against the other team—that's why you chose it as your game plan. What do you do?

Some would say, "Do what the boss says. You don't want him to get mad at you for insubordination." I disagree with that, however, and here's why.

Let's say you do what the boss asks, and you start to throw the ball in the second half, but your original assessment was right, passing doesn't work, and you lose the game. No big deal, right? At least you did what the boss said. However, by doing what the boss said, you sacrificed your long-term vision in favor of a short-term goal. If you do that enough times, you eventually will lose your vision of the entire season. You win a few, you lose a few, but now you have no vision, and therefore, no results.

As a result, what happens when you get to the end of the

season and the boss needs to renew your contract? He won't remember that the loss was his fault. Instead, he's going to look back at the season and say, "Another disappointing season; too many losses. We need a winning team if we want to sell tickets. It also seems like you don't have a clear direction for this team. We are not going to renew your contract."

The alternative is to disregard what the boss says and stick to your original vision. Your overall vision is to have a winning season and to make the playoffs, and your vision for this game—to run the football—helps you toward that overall vision. So stick to it. Sure, the boss will be furious, but if your vision was right to begin with, you should win the game. And if you win the game, the owner can't be that mad. Maybe you lose the game, maybe you win. At least you've stuck to your vision, and your players will see the vision and will buy in as well. Hopefully, at the end of the year, your leadership and your vision will shine through and the team will make the playoffs. And at that point, the owner will have forgotten your slight insubordination because you put a winning product on the field and you are selling tickets for him. That will result in a renewal of your contract.

Create a vision with the help of your peons. Figure out small steps to take you there. Present the vision to your employees, and stick to it.

A good, productive manager with a great vision must also remember that sometimes things cannot be changed overnight. I know you managers think things can and should be changed the minute you make adjustments. However, sometimes good growth takes time. I know that when you see problems, your gut reaction is to change everything immediately and get results right away. Please hold off on your gut reaction.

**Your gut is a place to store fat and belly lint; it's not a place to make wise decisions.**

Any good program, any effective change, may take months or years to manifest in your goal attainment. Plan for that. In the case of my Worst to First plan, for example, the goal wasn't centered on "Worst to First by Friday," it was "by May 31st," a goal that spanned an entire year. Don't get flustered if things haven't turned around within a week of making a change. Don't assume that the change was a bad move and suddenly make another change. Sometimes, as Spencer and I found in our feeble attempt in the Turkey Trot race, changes that put you in first right away are not the kind of changes that are going to sustain you.

### Keep it All Together

Now that we've discussed organization as a means to help your team reach a vision while avoiding the trap of being a "flavor of the month," it must also be discussed as a way to help you maintain a peon-manager relationship. Throughout this book, we have discussed many great ways to build a more personal, trusting relationship with your employees. I've suggested many ways to accomplish this, such as getting to know personal elements of your peons' lives, remembering their birthdays, and getting to know what really drives your people.

It is important to stay organized in your new, personal relationship with your peons. Just think how you'd feel if every Monday your manager came up to you and asked your spouse's name, the same question every week: you would infer that the manager wasn't really interested in the answer. On the other hand, how different would your reaction be if, after not talking to your manager for a month, he came up to you and said, "So how is [your husband] John doing? How is he liking working at FDM International?" You would probably be very impressed, to say the least. The way for you to be the kind of manager that remembers all those details of your peons' lives is to get organized, to keep it all together.

How do you file your work materials for quick reference? Do you use manila folders and a filing cabinet? Do you just create folders on a computer? Whichever way you do it, you need to use that same organized system for managing your relationship with your peons.

I once had a very effective manager in a church setting. When I was nineteen, I volunteered my time and spent two years as a missionary in Argentina. I was part of a geographic mission that consisted of about 180 to 200 missionaries. Each month, ten or fifteen missionaries would head home and an equal number would arrive in the country. This mission was organized into a handful of zones, all led by peer managers, and only one person was designated as an official manager. He was responsible for the education, morale, and organization of these two hundred missionaries, all the while losing ten or so each month and picking up ten new ones. Not an easy task, by anyone's standards.

The manager assigned to my area of Argentina, we will call him "El Presidente," was very organized. He held monthly meetings with the members of each zone as a whole, and he also held monthly one-on-one interviews with each person in his organization—all two hundred, every month. And each month, most of those two hundred people came to him with either concerns or questions.

In order to handle all his tasks, El Presidente carried a laptop computer around with him, and he kept a file on his computer for each individual missionary. Every time he met with a specific missionary, he pulled up their file and had an instant record of all the things they had discussed previously. If I told him one month that I was concerned because I was having trouble speaking Spanish, he would jot it down in the laptop. Then, the next month when I met with him, the first thing he would ask was, "How is the Spanish coming along?"

I was not offended in the slightest that his memory happened to be carried in a portable computer. In fact, I found it very comforting to know he cared enough to put our conversations in his laptop. I found it refreshing to see El Presidente strive to remember personal elements about others and about me. It was also nice because he didn't have to ask me the same probing questions every month, over and over again.

Remember, it is a good idea to know about your peons' personal lives, and a computer file is a very handy way to remember a spouse's name, or a birthday, or a peon's aspirations. Or use your day planner, a spreadsheet on your PDA—even a yellow pad stored in a filing cabinet. Wouldn't that be a great tool to have every time you had to have a performance review? Wouldn't you love to be able to look at minutes from the last meeting you had with that person, just before meeting with them again? Can you imagine the look on that peon's face when you ask, "So how are your kids Chump and Mutt doing? Isn't your wedding anniversary coming up this month? Have you gotten a gift yet? And what is Poodles up to these days? Did you ever figure out how to get him to stop digging holes?"

The peons will be floored. They'll wonder who you've been talking to. They'll probably feel embarrassed that they don't know *your* dog's name. Getting organized in your relationships with your peons is the only way to implement all of the suggestions we've discussed in this book. Getting organized will help you gain the trust of your employees and will help you be more personal with them. They will also see that you are striving to understand their work, and they will be more likely to give you feedback if they see you handle it in an organized fashion.

A great way to do that is by creating some sort of spreadsheet, placed in either a filing cabinet or a computer file, with columns for each employee's name, their spouse's name (if they have one), maybe their kids' or their pets' names, their family situation growing up, their hobbies or interests, their career goals or plans within the company, and what you last talked about with them. Basically, create a contact management database. It doesn't have to include all kinds of frills, just the critical information. I understand that a computer is the last place some people feel organized, and that's fine. The point is that you need to get organized, using whatever method works best for you. The method does not matter. Just get organized. It's fun, it's easy, and it's worth it.

Then, every so often, review it all. Particularly the column that reminds you what you talked about with that person yesterday. If you promised to do the paperwork for a peon's tuition reimbursement, do it. If you can't do it, deliberately go to them and tell them you are working on it. If you asked them yesterday how many sales they have this week, don't ask them again today—find another productive topic to ask about. If you asked them about their kids yesterday, ask them about their spouse today—and listen to the answer.

I've presented some good suggestions in this book. Some were even great suggestions, if I may say so myself. Organization is the tool that will help you implement these suggestions. Getting organized in your vision, in the stability of that vision, and in your relationships with your peons will help you to change your focus, to go from the manager you are today to the more effective, peon-centered manager of tomorrow.

### Conclusion: To Change or Not to Change?

In the world of winter mountain sports, there are basically two types of people: skiers and snowboarders. Skiers prefer the traditional method of sliding down the mountain, with a plank on each foot. Skiing is thousands of years old and practiced all over the world by people young and old. Snowboarders, on the other hand, prefer to break from the norm, sliding down mountains on a single plank, sideways. Although it has gained popularity and acceptance in the past ten or fifteen years, snowboarding is still viewed as a bit unconventional. If winter sports were desserts, skiing would be a banana split, and snowboarding would be more like rainbow sherbet with chocolate syrup and nuts on top, with a pickle on the side.

I learned how to ski when I was ten. It started with a quick tutorial, a bunny slope, and a wet pair of bibs. Soon, however, I developed a love for the sport—to be a skier in Arizona, you have to love the sport. I got to the point where I was very comfortable with my skill set as a skier. I'm not a Warren Miller–quality skier, but I do consider myself an expert.

So when some of my friends started to try out those new-fangled snowboards, I resisted. My excuse always was, "I don't want to waste a day of skiing to spend it learning how to snowboard." In other words, I didn't want to put myself back into a situation where I was a novice. Even though many people tried to convince me that snowboarding was a lot of fun, I resisted the temptation to get outside my expertise. It had taken a lot of practice and a lot of time recovering in a hot tub to get to my level of skiing expertise; I wasn't about to give that up to go back to being terrible again.

Eventually, I got married and had kids—and mysteriously had a hard time finding as much free time to ski. However, a couple years ago my younger brother invited me to join him on a trip up to the mountains to go skiing. "And," he said, "I can teach you to snowboard while we are up there." Not feeling the sense of ego I once felt as a skier, I agreed to let him instruct me in snowboarding.

The first morning was very painful. My knees felt like they were going to crumble any second, and I think I got a concussion (I can't quite remember). It almost got to the point where I told him, "This is stupid. Let's just go to the car and get my skis—I know I can do that." However, I trudged on, and at some point that afternoon, I began to get the hang of the snowboard. I was happy to put three simultaneous turns together, and I started to get a glimpse of the fun everybody had been telling me about. It was fun. It did feel cool. I started to enjoy it. Before long, the day was over, and my attempt at snowboarding was cut short.

Were it not for my brother inviting me and teaching me, I would never have taken the time to try something new. Were it not for my loss of ego, I would have turned down the opportunity to snowboard, just as I did every other time. Were it not for my willingness to learn, and to stick to the task even when it was very painful, I would never have felt the great sensation of riding a snowboard.

After reading this book, are you still a skier, or are you now thinking you might try snowboarding? Not in the literal sense, of course — I mean in the sense of your management style. Are you going to continue to do things the way you always have, to keep things comfortable? If you continue to do things the way they've always been done, you'll get the same results you've always gotten. If you do things like everyone else, you'll get the same results that they do. And maybe that's okay for you. Maybe the status quo is just fine. Maybe you're happy as a skier, and you don't want to try snowboarding, even if you might like it better — even if it might truly be a better way down the mountain.

Some of you may decide that you don't want to be a peon-centered manager. Others may already be practicing some elements of employee-centered leadership and only have some minor adjustments to make. For still others, it may just be a slight change in focus. Whatever the case, I challenge you to make that change. Be a peon manager. Practice equality in your management style. Focus on gaining and maintaining the trust of your peons. Be more personal. Spend time with them in the trenches. Beg for their feedback, and approach your managerial goals with a sense of purpose and organization.

This was your opportunity to look into the mind of the peon, to see what it is we peons expect you to do, how we peons expect to be treated, and how it is possible to get us peons to actually work. Take this information and do something with it. When you start to change your ways, I guarantee you will see a difference in your team's productivity and happiness, and a drop in voluntary turnover. It's really not that difficult, and my suggestions aren't groundbreaking—I realize that. Nonetheless, I hope my suggestions have helped you begin to change your focus. I hope you have been able to see your managerial work from a different point of view. And I hope you've learned that

**the best way to manage peons is to avoid treating them like peons**.

((

# Index

**A**

Attitude, importance of, 33

**B**

Birthdays, remembering, 20, 55–56, 63, 143–46
Boundary testing, 70

**C**

Catchphrases, 131–32
Change
    allowing time for, 141–42
    environment for, 147–49
    of management style, 149–50
Communication
    open, 23–27
    vision and, 137–38
Contact management databases, 146
Creative performing, 100–112

**D**

Deceit, 14, 30
Disrespect, 33–34, 41

**E**

Empathy
    definition of, 42–43
    lack of, 43–50
    showing, 50–52
Employees. See Peons
Equality, importance of, 34, 41–42

**F**

Fear
    feedback and, 117–18
    as motivator, 49–50
Feedback
    fear of, 117–18
    giving, 88–91, 96, 114
    importance of quality, 115, 116
    receiving, 3–4, 114–25
Focus, changing, 6–8, 62, 150

**G**

Goals
    meaningful, 129–31, 136–37
    of peons, focusing on, 62–64
    setting realistic, 100–112
    weekly, monthly, and yearly, 133–36
Gut reactions, 142

**H**

Holidays, 21–23
Honesty
    importance of, 18–19
    meeting production goals and, 102–12

**L**

Leadership by example, 80–81
Lunch, 97–98

**M**

Management
    dog training analogy for, 2–3
    imaginary gap between peons and, 33–41
    ladder, following, 96
    micro-, 47–50
Mom's key to, 53–54
Parent Theory of, 46–47
    revenue and, 99
    style, changing, 149–50
    ubiquity of, 54
Managers
    approachable, 59
    effective, 70–71
    equality of peons and, 41–42
    as people, 71–78
    performing peons' job functions, 81–95
    personality traits for, 13–19
    reciprocating relationship between peons and, 56–60
    suggestions for, 7–8
    two-faced, 27–29
    vacation and sick time for, 75–78

# Index

Micromanagement, 47–50
Motivation
    fear and, 49–50
    respect and, 31–32

## N

Names, remembering, 20, 55–56, 63–64, 143–46

## O

Open door policies, 3–4, 117
Organization
    effects of, 132
    importance of, 131, 146
    peon-manager relationship and, 142–46
    tidiness vs., 132–33
    vision and, 133–42

## P

Parent Theory, 46–47
Peons
    boundary testing by, 70
    definition of, viii–ix, 8–9
    earning trust of, 14–15, 19–27, 29–30
    empathizing with, 42–47
    equality of managers and, 41–42
    expectations of, 5
    focusing on goals of, 62–64
    imaginary gap between management and, 33–41
    managers performing job functions of, 81–95
    motivating, 31–32, 49
    as people, 45–46, 55–60
    quitting, 60–61
    reciprocating relationship between managers and, 56–60
    remembering names and birthdays of, 20, 55–56, 63–64, 143–46
    respecting, 31–32, 41–42
    satisfaction surveys of, 3–4

suggestions from, 118–21
Personality traits, 13–19
Policy enforcement, 64–70
Priorities, setting, 76–77
Productivity
    holidays and, 21–23
    increasing, 62–64, 100–112
Promises, unfulfilled, 29

## R

Remembering
    empathy as, 50–52
    names and birthdays, 20, 55–56
    tools for, 143–46
Respect
    motivation and, 32
    policy enforcement and, 70
Results, focusing on, 129–31
Rumors, avoiding, 24–25

## S

Sick time, 75
Steadiness, importance of, 19–20
Suggestion boxes, 124–25

## T

Terminations, 25–26
Threats
    effects of, 48–50
    unfulfilled, 29
Trust
    betraying, 27–29
    earning, 14–15, 19–27, 29–30
    importance of, 13–15, 30
    lack of, 15–18
Turnover, 60–61
Two-faced, appearing, 27–29

## V

Vacation time, 75–78
Vision
    communicating, 137–38
    creating, 133–37
    map or calendar of, 137
    sticking with original, 138–42

152

## About the Author

While working for a landscaping company at his first summer job, Dave Haynes learned the definition of peon when he was informed that he was not allowed to touch the lawnmowers, and was instead relegated to "weed-pickin'" duty. Lawnmowers were reserved for senior landscaping professionals.

Since then, he has noticed that the view from the bottom seems to be the same, no matter what the job. He has spent time as a lifeguard, a telemarketer (the real obnoxious kind), a school bus driver, a marketing professional, a pool guy, and a salesperson. One time he thought he had finally broken through when he was appointed Marketing Director for a small manufacturer. He soon found, however, that nothing had changed. He was still doing all the work, with no extra pay and no subordinates—just a title and some nice-looking business cards.

He now works in international sales for a Fortune 500 company. He's not going to tell you which one, because he wants to keep his job. Unless this book sells a million copies. Then he'll tell you.

Dave lives in Arizona with his wife Lorette, their two boys Caleb and Conner, and their two girls Nickelle and Haylee. Dave can be reached at peonguy@peonbook.com.

## Berrett-Koehler Publishers

B errett-Koehler is an independent publisher of books and other publications at the leading edge of new thinking and innovative practice on work, business, management, leadership, stewardship, career development, human resources, entrepreneurship, and global sustainability.

Since the company's founding in 1992, we have been committed to creating a world that works for all by publishing books that help us to integrate our values with our work and work lives, and to create more humane and effective organizations.

We have chosen to focus on the areas of work, business, and organizations, because these are central elements in many people's lives today. Furthermore, the work world is going through tumultuous changes, from the decline of job security to the rise of new structures for organizing people and work. We believe that change is needed at all levels—individual, organizational, community, and global—and our publications address each of these levels.

**To find out about** our new books,
special offers,
free excerpts,
and much more,
subscribe to our free monthly eNewsletter at

www.bkconnection.com

Please see next pages for other books
from Berrett-Koehler Publishers